GREAT BRITAIN AND HER QUEEN

ANNE E. KEELING

Great Britain and Her Queen

Anne E. Keeling

© 1st World Library, 2007
PO Box 2211
Fairfield, IA 52556
www.1stworldlibrary.com
First Edition

LCCN: 2007923743

Softcover ISBN: 978-1-4218-4226-4
Hardcover ISBN: 978-1-4218-4128-1
eBook ISBN: 978-1-4218-4324-7

Purchase *"Great Britain and Her Queen"*
as a traditional bound book at:
www.1stWorldLibrary.com/purchase.asp?ISBN=978-1-4218-4226-4

1st World Library is a literary, educational organization
dedicated to:

- Creating a free internet library of downloadable ebooks

- Hosting writing competitions and offering book publishing
scholarships.

Interested in more 1st World Library books? contact:
literacy@1stworldlibrary.com
Check us out at: www.1stworldlibrary.com

1st World Library Literary Society

Giving Back to the World

"If you want to work on the core problem, it's early school literacy."

- James Barksdale, former CEO of Netscape

"No skill is more crucial to the future of a child, or to a democratic and prosperous society, than literacy."

- Los Angeles Times

"Literacy... means far more than learning how to read and write... The aim is to transmit... knowledge and promote social participation."

- UNESCO

"Literacy is not a luxury, it is a right and a responsibility. If our world is to meet the challenges of the twenty-first century we must harness the energy and creativity of all our citizens."

- President Bill Clinton

"Parents should be encouraged to read to their children, and teachers should be equipped with all available techniques for teaching literacy, so the varying needs and capacities of individual kids can be taken into account."

- Hugh Mackay

CONTENTS

I. THE GIRL QUEEN AND HER KINGDOM.........................7

II. STORM AND SUNSHINE..22

III. FRANCE AND ENGLAND...39

IV. THE CRIMEAN WAR..47

V. INDIA 61

VI. THE BEGINNINGS OF SORROWS..............................74

VII. CHANGES GOOD AND EVIL.....................................91

VIII. OUR COLONIES...106

IX. INTELLECTUAL AND SPIRITUAL PROGRESS........114

X. PROGRESS OF THE EMPIRE FROM 1887 TO 1897....128

XI. PROGRESS OF WESLEYAN METHODISM
    UNDER QUEEN VICTORIA, 1837-1897......................139

CONCLUSION...176

CHAPTER I

THE GIRL-QUEEN AND HER KINGDOM

Rather more than one mortal lifetime, as we average life in these later days, has elapsed since that June morning of 1837, when Victoria of England, then a fair young princess of eighteen, was roused from her tranquil sleep in the old palace at Kensington, and bidden to rise and meet the Primate, and his dignified associates the Lord Chamberlain and the royal physician, who "were come on business of state to the Queen"—words of startling import, for they meant that, while the royal maiden lay sleeping, the aged King, whose heiress she was, had passed into the deeper sleep of death. It is already an often-told story how promptly, on receiving that summons, the young Queen rose and came to meet her first homagers, standing before them in hastily assumed wrappings, her hair hanging loosely, her feet in slippers, but in all her hearing such royally firm composure as deeply impressed those heralds of her greatness, who noticed at the same moment that her eyes were full of tears. This little scene is not only charming and touching, it is very significant, suggesting a combination of such qualities as are not always found united: sovereign good sense and readiness, blending with quick, artless feeling that sought no disguise—such feeling as again betrayed itself when on her ensuing proclamation the new Sovereign had to meet her people face to face, and stood before them at her palace window, composed but sad, the tears running unchecked down her fair pale face.

That rare spectacle of simple human emotion, at a time when a selfish or thoughtless spirit would have leaped in exultation, touched the heart of England deeply, and was rightly held of happy omen. The nation's feeling is aptly expressed in the glowing verse of Mrs. Browning, praying Heaven's blessing on the "weeping Queen," and prophesying for her the love, happiness, and honour which have been hers in no stinted measure. "Thou shalt be well beloved," said the poetess; there are very few sovereigns of whom it could be so truly said that they *have* been well beloved, for not many have so well deserved it. The faith of the singer has been amply justified, as time has made manifest the rarer qualities joyfully divined in those early days in the royal child, the single darling hope of the nation.

Once before in the recent annals of our land had expectations and desires equally ardent centred themselves on one young head. Much of the loyal devotion which had been alienated from the immediate family of George III. had transferred itself to his grandchild, the Princess Charlotte, sole offspring of the unhappy marriage between George, Prince of Wales, and Caroline of Brunswick. The people had watched with vivid interest the young romance of Princess Charlotte's happy marriage, and had bitterly lamented her too early death—an event which had overshadowed all English hearts with forebodings of disaster. Since that dark day a little of the old attachment of England to its sovereigns had revived for the frank-mannered sailor and "patriot king," William IV; but the hopes crushed by the death of the much-regretted Charlotte had renewed themselves with even better warrant for Victoria. She was the child of no ill-omened, miserable marriage, but of a fitting union; her parents had been sundered only by death, not by wretched domestic dissensions. People heard that the mortal malady which deprived her of a father had been brought about by the Duke of Kent's simple delight in his baby princess, which kept him playing with the child when he should have been changing his wet outdoor garb; and they found something touching and tender in the tragic little circumstance. And everything that could be noticed of the manner in which the bereaved duchess was training up her precious charge spoke well for the mother's wisdom and affection, and for the future of the daughter.

It was indeed a happy day for England when Edward, Duke of Kent, the fourth son of George III, was wedded to Victoria of Saxe-Coburg, the widowed Princess of Leiningen—happy, not only because of the admirable skill with which that lady conducted her illustrious child's education, and because of the pure, upright principles, the frank, noble character, which she transmitted to that child, but because the family connection established through that marriage was to be yet further serviceable to the interests of our realm. Prince Albert of Saxe-Coburg was second son of the Duchess of Kent's eldest brother, and thus first cousin of the Princess Victoria—"the Mayflower," as, in fond allusion to the month of her birth, her mother's kinsfolk loved to call her: and it has been made plain that dreams of a possible union between the two young cousins, very nearly of an age, were early cherished by the elders who loved and admired both.

The Princess's life, however, was sedulously guarded from all disturbing influences. She grew up in healthy simplicity and seclusion; she was not apprised of her nearness to the throne till she was twelve years old; she had been little at Court, little in sight, but had been made familiar with her own land and its history, having received the higher education so essential to her great position; while simple truth and rigid honesty were the very atmosphere of her existence. From such a training much might be hoped; but even those who knew most and hoped most were not quite prepared for the strong individual character and power of self-determination that revealed themselves in the girlish being so suddenly transferred "from the nursery to the throne." It was quickly noticed that the part of Queen and mistress seemed native to her, and that she filled it with not more grace than propriety. "She always strikes me as possessed of singular penetration, firmness, and independence," wrote Dr. Norman Macleod in 1860; acute observers in 1837 took note of the same traits, rarer far in youth than in full maturity, and closely connected with the "reasoning, searching" quality of her mind, "anxious to get at the root and reality of things, and abhorring all shams, whether in word or deed." [Footnote]

[Footnote: "Life of Norman Macleod, D.D." vol. ii.]

It was well for England that its young Sovereign could exemplify virile strength as well as womanly sweetness; for it was indeed a cloudy and dark day when she was called to her post of lonely grandeur and hard responsibility; and to fill that post rightly would have overtasked and over-whelmed a feebler nature. It is true that the peace of Europe, won at Waterloo, was still unbroken. But already, within our borders and without them, there were the signs of coming storm. The condition of Ireland was chronically bad; the condition of England was full of danger; on the Continent a new period of earth-shaking revolution announced itself not doubtfully.

It would be hardly possible to exaggerate the wretched state of the sister isle, where fires of recent hate were still smouldering, and where the poor inhabitants, guilty and

Anne E. Keeling

guiltless, were daily living on the verge of famine, over which they were soon to be driven. Their ill condition much aggravated by the intemperate habits to which despairing men so easily fall a prey. The expenditure of Ireland on proof spirits alone had in the year 1829 attained the sum of L6,000,000.

In England many agricultural labourers were earning starvation wages, were living on bad and scanty food, and were housed so wretchedly that they might envy the hounds their dry and clean kennels. A dark symptom of their hungry discontent had shown itself in the strange crime of rick-burning, which went on under cloud of night season after season, despite the utmost precautions which the luckless farmers could adopt. The perpetrators were not dimly guessed to be half-famished creatures, taking a mad revenge for their wretchedness by destroying the tantalising stores of grain, too costly for their consumption; the price of wheat in the early years of Her Majesty's reign and for some time previously being very high, and reaching at one moment (1847) the extraordinary figure of a hundred and two shillings per quarter.

There was threatening distress, too, in some parts of the manufacturing districts; in others a tolerably high level of wages indicated prosperity. But even in the more favoured districts there was needless suffering. The hours of work, unrestricted by law, were cruelly long; nor did there exist any restriction as to the employment of operatives of very tender years. "The cry of the children" was rising up to heaven, not from the factory only, but from the underground darkness of the mine, where a system of pitiless infant slavery prevailed, side by side with the employment of women as beasts of burden, "in an atmosphere of filth and profligacy." The condition of too many toilers was rendered more hopeless by the thriftless follies born of ignorance. The educational provision made by the piety of former ages was no longer adequate to the needs of the ever-growing nation; and all the voluntary efforts made by clergy and laity, by Churchmen and Dissenters, did not fill up the deficiency—a fact which had only just begun to meet with State recognition. It was in 1834 that Government first obtained from Parliament the grant of a small sum in aid of education. Under a defective system of poor-relief, recently reformed, an immense mass of idle pauperism had come into being; it still remained to be seen if a new Poor Law could do away with the mischief created by the old one.

Looking at the earliest years of Her Majesty's rule, the first impulse is to exclaim:

"And all this trouble did not pass, but grew."

It seemed as if poverty became ever more direful, and dissatisfaction more importunate. A succession of unfavourable seasons and failing crops produced extraordinary distress; and the distress in its turn was fruitful first of deepened discontent, and then of political disturbances. The working classes had looked for immediate relief from their burdens when the Reform Bill should be carried, and had striven hard to insure its success: it had been carried triumphantly in 1832, but no perceptible improvement in their lot had yet resulted; and a resentful feeling of disappointment and of being victims of deception now added bitterness to their blind sense of misery and injury, and greatly exasperated the political agitation of the ten stormy years that followed.

No position could well be more trying than that of the inexperienced girl who, in the first bloom of youth, was called to rule the land in this wild transitional period. Her royal courage and gracious tact, her transparent truthfulness, her high sense of duty, and her precocious discretion served her well; but these young excellences could not have produced their full effect had she not found in her first Prime Minister a faithful friend and servant, whose loyal and chivalrous devotion at once conciliated her regard, and who only used the influence thus won to impress on his Sovereign's mind "sound maxims of constitutional government, and truths of every description which it behoved her to learn." The records of the time show plainly that Lord Melbourne, the eccentric head of William IV's last Whig Administration, was not generally credited with either the will or the ability to play so lofty a part. His affectation of a lazy, trifling, indifferent manner, his often-quoted remonstrance to impetuous would-be reformers, "Can't you let it alone?" had earned for him some angry disapproval, and caused him to be regarded as the embodiment of the detested *laissez-faire* principle. But under his mask of nonchalance he hid some noble qualities, which at this juncture served Queen and country well.

Considered as a frivolous, selfish courtier by too many of the suffering poor and of their friends, he was in truth "acting in all things an affectionate, conscientious, and patriotic part" towards his Sovereign, "endeavouring to make her happy as a woman and popular as a Queen," [Footnote] telling her uncourtly truths with a blunt honesty that did not displease her, and watching over her with a paternal tenderness which she repaid with frank, noble confidence. He was faithful in a great and difficult trust; let his memory have due honour.

[Footnote: C. C. F. Greville: "A Journal of the Reign of Queen Victoria."]

Under Melbourne's pilotage the first months of the new reign went by with some serenity, though the political horizon remained threatening enough, and the temper of the nation appeared sullen. "The people of England seem inclined to hurrah no more," wrote Greville of one of the Queen's earliest public appearances, when "not a hat was raised nor a voice heard" among the coldly curious crowd of spectators. But the splendid show of her coronation a half-year later awakened great enthusiasm—enthusiasm most natural and inevitable. It was youth and grace and goodness, all the freshness and the infinite promise of spring, that wore the crimson and the ermine and the gold, that sat enthroned amid the ancient glories of the Abbey to receive the homage of all that was venerable and all that was great in a mighty kingdom, and that bowed in meek devotion to receive the solemn consecrating blessing of the Primate, according to the holy custom followed in England for a thousand years, with little or no variation since the time when Dunstan framed the Order of Coronation, closely following the model of the Communion Service. Some other features special to *this* coronation heightened the national delight in it. Its arrangements evidently had for their chief aim to interest and to gratify the people. Instead of the banquet in Westminster Hall, which could have been seen only by the privileged and the wealthy, a grand procession through London was arranged, including all the foreign ambassadors, and proceeding from Buckingham Palace to Westminster Abbey by a route two or three miles in length, so that the largest possible number of spectators might enjoy the magnificent pageant. And the overflowing multitudes whose dense masses lined the whole long way, and in whose tumultuous cheering pealing bells and sounding trumpets and thundering cannon were almost unheard as the young Queen passed through the shouting ranks, formed themselves the most impressive spectacle to the half-hostile foreign witnesses, who owned that the sight of these rejoicing thousands of freemen was grand indeed, and impossible save in that England which, then as now, was not greatly loved by its rivals. An element which appealed powerfully to the national pride and the

Anne E. Keeling

national generosity was supplied by the presence of the Duke of Wellington and of Marshal Soult, his old antagonist, who appeared as French ambassador. Soult, as he advanced with the air of a veteran warrior, was followed by murmurs of admiring applause, which swelled into more than murmurs for the hero of Waterloo bending in homage to his Sovereign. A touch of sweet humanity was added to the imposing scene within the Abbey through what might have been a painful accident. Lord Rolle, a peer between seventy and eighty years of age, stumbling and falling as he climbed the steps of the throne, the Queen impulsively moved as if to aid him; and when the old man, undismayed, persisted in carrying out his act of homage, she asked quickly, "May I not get up and meet him?" and descended one or two steps to save him the ascent. The ready natural kindliness of the royal action awoke ecstatic applause, which could hardly have been heartier had the applauders known how true a type that act supplied of Her Majesty's future conduct. She has never feared to peril her dignity by descending a step or two from her throne, when "sweet mercy, nobility's true badge," has seemed to require such a descent. And her queenly dignity has never been thereby lessened. "She never ceases to be a Queen," says Greville *a propos* of this scene, "and is always the most charming, cheerful, obliging, unaffected Queen in the world."

That "the people" were more considered in the arrangements for this coronation than they had been on any previous occasion of the sort was a circumstance quite in harmony with certain other signs of the times. "The night is darkest before the dawn," and amid all the gloom which enshrouded the land there could be discerned the stir and movement that herald the coming of the day. Men's minds were turning more and more to the healing of the world's wounds. Already one great humane enterprise had been carried through in the emancipation of the slaves in British Colonies; already the vast work of prison reform had been well begun, through the saintly Elizabeth Fry, whose life of faithful service ended ere the Queen had reigned eight years. The very year of Her Majesty's accession was signalised by two noteworthy endeavours to put away wrong. We will turn first to that which *seems* the least immediately philanthropic, although the injustice which it remedied was trivial in appearance only, since in its everyday triviality it weighed most heavily on the most numerous class—that of the humble and the poor.

How would the Englishman of to-day endure the former exactions of the Post Office? The family letters of sixty years ago, written on the largest sheets purchasable, crossed and crammed to the point of illegibility, filled with the news of many and many a week, still witness of the time when "a letter from London to Brighton cost eightpence, to Aberdeen one and threepence-halfpenny, to Belfast one and four-pence"; when, "if the letter were written on more than one sheet, it came under the operation of a higher scale of charges," and when the privilege of franking letters, enjoyed and very largely exercised by members of Parliament and members of the Government, had the peculiar effect of throwing the cost of the mail service exactly on that part of the community which was least able to bear it. The result of the injustice was as demoralising as might have been expected. The poorer people who desired to have tidings of distant friend or relative were driven by the prohibitory rates of postage into all sorts of curious, not quite honest devices, to gratify their natural desire without being too heavily taxed for it. A brother and sister, for instance, unable to afford themselves the costly luxury of regular correspondence, would obtain assurance of each other's well-being by transmission through the post at stated intervals of blank papers duly sealed and addressed: the arrival of the postman with a missive of this kind announced to the recipient that all

Anne E. Keeling

was well with the sender, so the unpaid "letter" was cheerfully left on the messenger's hands. Such an incident, coming under the notice of Mr. Rowland Hill, impressed him with a sense of hardship and wrong in the system that bore these fruits; and he set himself with strenuous patience to remedy the wrong and the hardship. His scheme of reform was worked out and laid before the public early in 1837; in the third year of Her Majesty's reign it was first adopted in its entirety, with what immense profit to the Government we may partly see when we contrast the seventy-six or seventy-seven millions of *paid* letters delivered in the United Kingdom during the last year of the heavy postage with the number exceeding a thousand millions, and still increasing— delivered yearly during the last decade; while the population has not doubled. That the Queen's own letters carried postage under the new regime was a fact almost us highly appreciated as Her Majesty's voluntary offer at a later date to bear her due share of the income tax.

It is well to notice how later Postmasters General, successors of Rowland Hill in that important office, have striven further to benefit their countrymen. In particular, Henry Fawcett's earnest efforts to encourage and aid habits of thrift are worthy of remembrance.

Again, it is during the first year of Her Majesty's reign that we find Father Mathew, the Irish Capuchin friar, initiating his vast crusade against intemperance, and by the charm of his persuasive eloquence and unselfish enthusiasm inducing thousands upon thousands to forswear the drink-poison that was destroying them. In two years he succeeded in enrolling two million five hundred thousand persons on the side of sobriety. The permanence of the good Father's immediate work was impaired by the superstitions which his poor followers associated with it, much against his desire. Not only were the medals which he gave as badges to his vowed abstainers regarded as infallible talismans from the hand of a saint, but the giver was credited with miraculous powers such as only a Divine Being could exercise, and which he disclaimed in vain—extravagances too likely to discredit his enterprise with more soberly judging persons than the imaginative Celts who were his earliest converts. But, notwithstanding every drawback, his action was most important, and deserves grateful memory. We may see in it the inception of that great movement whose indirect influence in reforming social habits and restraining excess had at least equalled its direct power for good on its pledged adherents. Though it is still unhappily true that drunkenness slays its tens of thousands among us, and largely helps to people our workhouses, our madhouses, and our gaols, yet the fiend walks not now, as it used to do, in unfettered freedom. It is no longer a fashionable vice, excused and half approved as the natural expression of joviality and good-fellowship; peers and commoners of every degree no longer join daily in the "heavy-headed revel" whose deep-dyed stain seems to have soaked through every page of our last-century annals. And it would appear as though the vice were not only held from increasing, but were actually on the decrease. The statistics of the last decade show that the consumption of alcohol is diminishing, and that of true food-stuffs proportionally rising.

There were other enterprises now set on foot, by no means directly philanthropic in their aim, which contemplated utility more than virtue or justice—enterprises whose vast effects are yet unexhausted, and which have so modified the conditions of human existence as to make the new reign virtually a new epoch. As to the real benefit of these immense changes, opinion is somewhat divided; but the majority would doubtless vote in their favour. The first railway in England, that between Liverpool and Manchester, had been opened in 1830, the day of its opening being made

Anne E. Keeling

darkly memorable by the accident fatal to Mr. Huskisson, as though the new era must be inaugurated by a sacrifice. Three years later there was but this one railway in England, and one, seven miles long, in Scotland. But in 1837 the Liverpool and Birmingham line was opened; in 1838 the London and Birmingham and the Liverpool and Preston lines, and an Act was passed for transmitting the mails by rail; in 1839 there was the opening of the London and Croydon line. The ball was set fairly rolling, and the supersession of ancient modes of communication was a question of time merely. The advance of the new system was much accelerated at the outset by the fact that railway enterprise became the favourite field for speculation, men being attracted by the novelty and tempted by exaggerated prospects of profit; and the mania was followed, like other manias, with results largely disastrous to the speculators and to commerce. But through years of good fortune and of bad fortune the iron network has continued to spread itself, until all the land lies embraced in its ramifications; and it is spreading still, like some strange organism the one condition of whose life is reproduction, knitting the greatest centres of commerce with the loneliest and remotest villages that were wont to lie far out of the travelled ways of men, and bringing *Ultima Thule* into touch with London.

Meanwhile the steam service by sea has advanced almost with that by land. In 1838 three steamships crossed the Atlantic between this country and New York, the *Great Western*, sailing from Bristol, and *Sirius*, from Cork, distinguished themselves by the short passages they made,— of fifteen days in the first case, and seventeen days in the second,—and by their using steam power *alone* to effect the transit, an experiment that had not been risked before. It was now proved feasible, and in a year or two there was set on foot that regular steam communication between the New World and the Old, which ever since has continued to draw them into always closer connection, as the steamers, like swift-darting shuttles, weave their multiplying magic lines across the liquid plain between.

The telegraph wires that run beside road and rail, doing the office of nerves in transmitting intelligence with thrilling quickness from the extremities to the head and from the head to the extremities of our State, are now so familiar an object, and their operations, such mere matters of every day, that we do not often recall how utterly unfamiliar they were sixty years ago, when Wheatstone and Cooke on this side the Atlantic, and Morse on the other, were devising their methods for giving signals and sounding alarms in distant places by means of electric currents transmitted through metallic circuits. Submarine telegraphy lay undreamed of in the future, land telegraphy was but just gaining hearing as a practicable improvement, when the crown was set on Her Majesty's head amid all that pomp and ceremony at Westminster. A modern English imagination is quite unequal to the task of realising the manifold hindrances that beset human intercourse at that day, when a journey by coach between places as important and as little remote from each other as Leeds and Newcastle occupied sixteen mortal hours, with changes of horses and stoppages for meals on the road, and when letters, unless forwarded by an "express" messenger at heavy cost, tarried longer on the way than even did passengers; while some prudent dwellers in the country deemed it well to set their affairs in order and make their wills before embarking on the untried perils of a journey up to town. These days are well within the memory of many yet living; but if the newer generations that have arisen during the present reign would understand what it is to be hampered in their movements and their correspondence as were their fathers, they must seek the remoter and more savage quarters of Europe, the less travelled portions of America or of half-explored Australia; they must plunge into Asian or African

Anne E. Keeling

wilds, untouched by civilisation, where as yet there runs not the iron horse, worker of greater marvels than the wizard steeds of fairy fable, that could, transport a single favoured rider over wide distances in little time. The subjugated, serviceable nature-power Steam, with its fellow-servant the tamed and tutored Lightning, has wonderfully contracted distance during these fifty years, making the earth, once so vast to human imagination, appear as a globe shrunken to a tenth of its ancient size, and bringing nations divided by half the surface of that globe almost within sound of each other's speech.

That there is damage as well as profit in all these increased facilities of intercourse must be apparent, since there is evil as well as good in the human world, and increased freedom of communication implies freer communication of the evil as of the good. But we may well hope that the cause of true upward progress will be most served by the vast inevitable changes which, as they draw all peoples nearer together, must deepen and strengthen the sense of human brotherhood, and, as they bring the deeds of all within the knowledge of all, must consume by an intolerable blaze of light the once secret iniquities and oppressions abhorrent to the universal conscience of mankind. The public conscience in these realms at least is better informed and more sensitive than it was in the year of William IV's death and of Victoria's accession.

CHAPTER II

STORM AND SUNSHINE

The beneficent changes we have briefly described were but just inaugurated, and their possible power for good was as yet hardly divined, when the young Queen entered into that marriage which we may well deem the happiest action of her life, and the most fruitful of good to her people, looking to the extraordinary character of the husband of her choice, and to the unobtrusive but always advantageous influence which his great and wise spirit exercised on our national life.

The marriage had been anxiously desired, and the way for it judiciously prepared, but it was in no sense forced on either of the contracting parties by their elders who so desired it. Prince Albert of Saxe-Coburg, second son of the Duke of Saxe-Coburg-Saalfeld, the Queen's maternal uncle, was nearly of an age with his royal cousin; he had already, young as he was, given evidence of a rare superiority of nature; he had been excellently trained; and there is no doubt that Leopold, king of the Belgians, his uncle, and the Queen's, did most earnestly desire to see the young heiress of the British throne, for whom he had a peculiar tenderness, united to the one person whose position and whose character combined to point him out as the fit partner for her high and difficult destinies. What tact, what patience, and what power

Anne E. Keeling

of self-suppression the Queen of England's husband would need to exercise, no one could better judge than Leopold, the widowed husband of Princess Charlotte; no one could more fully have exemplified these qualities than the prince in whom Leopold's penetration divined them.

The cousins had already met, in 1836, when their mutual attraction had been sufficiently strong; and in 1839, when Prince Albert, with his elder brother Ernest, was again visiting England, the impression already produced became ineffaceably deep. The Queen, whom her great rank compelled to take the initiative, was not very long in making up her mind when and how to act. Her favoured suitor himself, writing to a dear relative, relates how she performed the trying task, inviting him to render her intensely happy by making "the *sacrifice* of sharing her life with her, for she said she looked on it as a sacrifice. The joyous openness with which she told me this enchanted me, and I was quite carried away by it." This was on October 15th; nearly six weeks after, on November 23rd, she made to her assembled Privy Council the formal declaration of her intended marriage. There is something particularly touching in even the driest description of this scene; the betrothed bride wearing a simple morning dress, having on her arm a bracelet containing Prince Albert's portrait, which helped to give her courage; her voice, as she read the declaration clear, sweet, and penetrating as ever, but her hands trembling so excessively that it was surprising she could read the paper she held. It was a trying task, but not so difficult as that which had devolved on her a short time before, when, in virtue of her sovereign rank, she had first to speak the words of fate that bound her to her suitor.

Endowed with every charm of person, mind, and manner that can win and keep affection, Prince Albert was able, in marrying the Queen, who loved him and whom he loved, to secure for her a happiness rare in any rank, rarest of all on the cold heights of royalty. This was not all; he was the worthy partner of her greatness. Himself highly cultivated in every sense, he watched with keenest interest over the advance of all cultivation in the land of his adoption, and identified himself with every movement to improve its condition. His was the soul of a statesman—wide, lofty, far-seeing, patient; surveying all great things, disdaining no small things, but with tireless industry pursuing after all necessary knowledge. Add to these intellectual excellences the moral graces of ideal purity of life, chivalrous faithfulness of heart, magnanimous self-suppression, and fervent piety, and we have a slight outline of a character which, in the order of Providence, acted very strongly and with a still living force on the destinies of nineteenth-century England. The Queen had good reasons for the feeling of "confidence and comfort" that shone in the glance she turned on her bridegroom as they walked away, man and wife at last, from the altar of the Chapel Royal, on February 10th, 1840. The union she then entered into immeasurably enhanced her popularity, and strengthened her position as surely as it expanded her nature. Not many years elapsed before Sir Robert Peel could tell her that, in spite of the inroads of democracy, the monarchy had never been safer, nor had any sovereign been so beloved, because "the Queen's domestic life was so happy, and its example so good." Only the Searcher of hearts knoweth how great has been the holy power of a pure, fair, and noble example constantly shining in the high places of the land.

It was hinted by the would-be wise, in the early days of Her Majesty's married life, that it would be idle to look for the royally maternal feeling of an Elizabeth towards her people in a wedded constitutional sovereign. The judgment was a mistake. The formal limitations of our Queen's prerogative, sedulously as she has respected them, have never destroyed her sense of responsibility; wifehood and motherhood have not contracted her sympathies, but have deepened and widened them. The very sorrows of her domestic life have knit her in fellowship with other mourners. No great calamity can befall her humblest subjects, and she hear of it, but there comes the answering flash of tender pity. She is more truly the mother of her people, having walked on a level with them, and with "Love, who is of the valley," than if she had chosen to dwell alone and aloof.

For some years after her marriage the Queen's private life shows like a little isle of brightness in the midst of a stormy sea. Within and without our borders there was small prospect of settled peace at the very time of that marriage. We have said that Lord Melbourne was still Premier; but he and his Ministry had resigned office in the previous May, and had only come back to it in consequence of a curious misunderstanding known as "the Bedchamber difficulty." Sir Robert Peel, who was summoned to form a Ministry on Melbourne's defeat and resignation, had asked from Her Majesty the dismissal of two ladies of her household, the wives of prominent members of the departing Whig Government; but his request conveyed to her mind the sense that he designed to deprive her of all her actual attendants, and against this imagined proposal she set herself energetically. "She could not consent to a course which she conceived to be contrary to usage, and which was repugnant to her feelings." Peel on his part remained firm in his opinion as to the real necessity for the change which he had advocated. From the deadlock produced by mere misunderstanding there seemed at the time only one way of escaping; the defeated Whig Government returned to office. But Ministers who resumed power only because, "as gentlemen," they felt bound to do so, had little chance of retaining it. In September 1841, Lord Melbourne was superseded in the premiership by Sir Robert Peel, and then gave a final proof how single-minded was his loyal devotion by advising the new Prime Minister as to the tone and style likely to commend him to their royal mistress—a tone of clear straightforwardness. "The Queen," said Melbourne—who knew of what he was speaking, if any statesman then did—"is not conceited; she is aware there are many things she cannot understand, and likes them explained to her elementarily, not at length and in detail, but shortly and clearly." The counsel was given and was accepted with equal good feeling, such as was honourable to all concerned; and the Sovereign learned, as years went on, to repose a singular confidence in the Minister with whom her first relations had been so unpropitious, but whose real honesty, ability, and loyalty soon approved themselves to her clear perceptions, which no prejudice has long been able to obscure.

We are told that in later years Her Majesty referred to the disagreeable incident we have just related as one that could not have occurred, if she had had beside her Prince Albert "to talk to and employ in explaining matters," while she refused the suggestion that her impulsive resistance had been advised by any one about her. "It was entirely my own foolishness," [Footnote] she is said to have added—words breathing that perfect simplicity of candour which has always been one of her most strongly marked characteristics.

[Footnote: "Greville Memoirs," Third Part, vol. i.]

Though the matter caused a great sensation at the time, and gave rise to some dismal prophesyings, it was of no permanent importance, and is chiefly noted here because it throws a strong light on Her Majesty's need of such an ever-present aid as she had now secured in the husband wise beyond his years, who well understood his constitutional position, and was resolute to keep within it, avoiding entanglement with any party, and fulfilling with equal impartiality

Anne E. Keeling

and ability the duties of private secretary to his Sovereign-wife.

The Melbourne Ministry had had to contend with difficulties sufficiently serious, and of these the grimmest and greatest remained still unsettled. At the outset of the reign a rebellion in Canada had required strong repression; and we had taken the first step on a bad road by entering into those disputes as to our right to force the opium traffic on China, which soon involved us in a disastrously successful war with that country. On the other hand, our Indian Government had begun an un-called-for interference with the affairs of Afghanistan, which, successful at first, resulted in a series of humiliating reverses to our arms, culminating in one of the most terrible disasters that have ever befallen a British force—the wholesale massacre of General Elphinstone's defeated and retreating army on its passage through the terrible mountain gorge known as the Pass of Koord Cabul. It was on January 13th, 1842, that the single survivor of this massacre appeared, a half-fainting man, drooping over the neck of his wearied pony, before the fort of Jellalabad, which General Sale still held for the English. He only was "escaped alone" to tell the hideous tale. The ill-advised and ill-managed enterprise which thus terminated had extended over more than three years, had cost us many noble lives, in particular that of the much-lamented Alexander Burnes, had condemned many English women and children to a long and cruel captivity among the savage foe, and had absolutely failed as to the object for which it was undertaken—the instalment of Shah Soojah, a mere British tool, as ruler of Afghanistan, in place of the chief desired by the Afghan people, Dost Mahomed. When the disasters to our arms had been retrieved, as retrieved they were with exemplary promptness, and when the surviving prisoners were redeemed from their hard captivity, it was deemed sound policy for us to attempt no longer to "force a sovereign on a reluctant people," and to remain content with that limit which "nature appears to have assigned" to our Indian empire on its north-western border. Later adventures in the same field have not resulted so happily as to prove that these views were incorrect. Our prestige was seriously damaged in Hindostan by this first Afghan war, and was only partially re-established in the campaign against the Sikhs several years later, despite the dramatic grandeur of that "piece of Indian history" which resulted in our annexation of the Punjaub in 1846—a solid advantage balanced by the unpleasant fact that English soldiers had been proved not invincible by natives.

It will thus appear that there was not too much that was glorious or encouraging in our external affairs in these early years; but the internal condition of the country was never less reassuring. The general discontent of the English lower orders was taking shape as Chartism—a movement which could not have arisen but for the fierce suspicion with which the working classes had learnt to regard those who seemed their superiors in wealth, in rank, or in political power, and which the higher orders retaliated in dislike and distrust of the labouring population, whom they considered as seditious enemies of order and property. The demon of class hatred was never more alive and busy than in the decade which terminated in 1848.

"The Charter," which was the watchword of hope to so many, and the very war-note of discord to many more, comprised six points, of which some at least were sufficiently absurd, while others have virtually passed into law, quietly and naturally, in due course of time; and if the universal Age of Gold which ignorant Chartists looked for has not ensued, at least the anarchy and ruin which their opponents associated with the dreaded scheme are equally non-existent. So fast has the time moved that there is now a

Anne E. Keeling

little difficulty in understanding the passionate hopes with which the Charter was associated on the one side, and the panic which it inspired on the other; and there is much to move wondering compassion in the profound ignorance which those hopes betrayed, and the not inferior misery amid which they were cherished. Few persons are now so credulous as to expect that annual Parliaments or stipendiary members would insure the universal reign of peace and justice; the people have already found that vote by ballot and suffrage all but universal have neither equalised wealth nor abrogated greed and iniquity; and though there be some dreamers in our midst to-day who look for wonderful transformations of society to follow on possible reforms, there is not even in these dreamy schemes the same amazing disproportion of means to be employed and end to be attained as characterised the Chartist delusion.

In Ireland men were reposing unbounded faith in another sort of political panacea for every personal and social evil—the Repeal of the Union with England, advocated by Daniel O'Connell, with all the power of his passionate Celtic eloquence, and supported by all his extraordinary personal influence. Apparently he hoped to carry this agitation to the same triumphant issue as that for Catholic emancipation, in which he had taken a conspicuous part; but the new movement did not, like the old one, appeal immediately and plausibly to the English sense of fair play and natural justice. A competent and not unfriendly observer has remarked that O'Connell's "theory and policy were that Ireland was to be saved by a dictatorship entrusted to himself." Whether any salvation for the unhappy land did lie in such a dictatorship was a point on which opinion might well be divided. English opinion was massively hostile to it; but for years all the political enthusiasm of Ireland centred in O'Connell and the cause he upheld. The country might be on the brink of ruin and starvation, but the peril seemed forgotten while the dream lasted. The agitator was wont to refer to the Queen in terms of extravagant loyalty, and it would seem that the feeling was largely shared by his followers. However futile and vainglorious his scheme and methods may appear, we must not deny to him a distinction, rare indeed among Irish agitators, of having steadily disclaimed violence and advocated orderly and peaceable proceedings. He thought his cause would be injured, and not advanced, by such outrages as before and since his day have too often disgraced party warfare in Ireland. His favourite maxim was that "the man who commits a crime gives strength to the enemy." This opinion was not heartily endorsed by all his followers. When it became clear that his dislike of physical force was real, when he did not defy the Government, at last stirred into hostile action by the demonstrations he organised, there was an end of his power over the fiercer spirits whom he had roused against the rule of "the Saxon"—luckless phrase with which he had enriched the Anglo-Irish controversy, and misleading as luckless. O'Connell died, a broken and disappointed man, on his way to Rome in 1847; but the spirit he had raised and could not rule did not die with him, and the younger, more turbulent leaders, who had outbid him for popular approval, continued their anti-English warfare with growing zeal until the year of fate 1848.

Even the Principality of Wales had its own peculiar form of agitation, sometimes accompanied by outrage, during these wild opening years. The farmers and labourers in Wales were unprosperous and poor, and in the season of their adversity they found turnpikes and tolls multiplying on their public roads. They resented what appeared a cruel imposition with wrathful impatience, and ere long gave expression to their anger in wild deeds. A text of Scripture suggested to them a fantastic form of riot. They found that it was said of old to Rebecca, "Let thy seed possess the gate of those which hate them," and ere long "Rebecca and her children," men

Anne E. Keeling

masking in women's clothes, made fierce war by night on the "gates" they detested, destroying the turnpikes and driving out their keepers. These raids were not always bloodless. The Government succeeded in repressing the rioting, and then, finding that a real grievance had caused it, did away with the oppressive tolls, and dealt not too hardly with the captured offenders; leniency which soon restored Wales to tranquillity.

A peaceful, strictly constitutional, and finally successful agitation ran its steady course in England for several years contemporaneously with those we have already enumerated. The Anti-Corn-Law League, with which the names of Cobden and Bright are united as closely as those two distinguished men were united in friendship, had in 1838 found a centre eminently favourable to its operations in Manchester. Its leaders were able, well-informed, and upright men, profoundly convinced that their cause was just, and that the welfare of the people was involved in their success or failure. They were men of the middle class, acquainted intimately with the needs and doings of the trading community to which they belonged, and therefore at once better qualified to argue on questions affecting commerce, and less directly interested in the prosperity of agriculture, than the more aristocratic leaders of the nation. Both persuasive and successful speakers, one of them supremely eloquent, they were able to interest even the lowest populace in questions of political economy, and to make Free Trade in Corn the idol of popular passion. Their mode of agitation was eminently reasonable and wise; but it *was* an agitation, exciting wild enthusiasm and fierce opposition, and must be reckoned not among the forces tending to quiet, but among those that aroused anxious care in the first nine years of the reign. And it was a terrible calamity that at last placed victory within their grasp. The blight on the potato first showed itself in 1845—a new, undreamed-of disaster, probably owing to the long succession of unfavourable seasons. And the potato blight meant almost certainly famine in Ireland, where perhaps three-fourths of the population had no food but this root. The food supply of a whole nation seemed on the point of being cut off. A loud demand was made for "the opening of the ports." By existing laws the ports admitted foreign grain tinder import duties varying in severity inversely with the fluctuating price of home-grown grain; thus a certain high level in the cost of corn was artificially maintained. These regulations, though framed for the protection of the native producer, did not bear so heavily on the consumer as the law of 1815 which they replaced; and the principle represented by them had a large following in the country. But now the argument from famine proved potent to decide the wavering convictions of some who had long been identified with the cause of Protection. The champions of Free Trade were sure of triumph when Sir Robert Peel became one of their converts; and the Corn Bill which he carried in the June of 1846, granting with some little reserve and delay the reforms which the Anti-Corn-Law League had been formed to secure, brought that powerful association to a quiet end. But the threatening Irish famine and the growing Irish disturbances remained, to embarrass the Ministry of Lord John Russell, which came into power within less than a week of that great success of the Tory Minister, defeated on a question of Irish polity on the very day when his Corn Bill received the assent of the House of Lords.

We must not omit, as in passing we chronicle this singular fortune of a great Minister, to notice the grief with which Her Majesty viewed this turn of events. Amid all the anxiety of the period, amid her distress at the cruel sufferings of her servants in India, in Britain, in Ireland, and her care for their relief, she had had two sources of consolation: the pure and simple bliss of her home-life, and the assistance of two most valued counsellors—her husband and her Prime Minister.

Anne E. Keeling

One was inseparably at her side, but one must now leave it; and she and the Prince met their inevitable loss with the dignified outward acquiescence that was fitting, but with sorrow not less real. The Queen would have bestowed on Peel as distinguished an honour as she could confer—the Order of the Garter; Peel deemed it best to decline it gratefully. "He was from the people and of the people," and wished so to remain, content if his Queen could say, "You have been a faithful servant, and have done your duty to the country and to myself."

In hapless Ireland, torn by agitation and scourged by pestilence and famine, the general misery had reached a point where no fiscal measures, however wise, could at once alleviate it. The potato famine held on its dreadful way, and the darkest moment of Irish history seemed reached in the year when one hundred and seventy thousand persons perished in that island by hunger or hunger-bred fever. The new plague affected Great Britain also; but its suffering was completely overshadowed by the enormous bulk of Irish woe, which the utmost lavishness of charity seemed scarcely to lessen. That there should be turbulence and even violence accompanying all this wretchedness was no way surprising; but in most men's minds the wretchedness held the larger place, and deservedly so, for the sedition, when ripe enough, was dealt with sharply, though not mercilessly, in such a way that ere long all reasonable dread of a civil war being added to the other horrors, had passed away; and the country had leisure for such recovery as was possible to a land so desolate.

There was contemporaneous distress enough and to spare in Great Britain: failures in Lancashire alone to the amount of L16,000,000; failures equally heavy in Birmingham, Glasgow, and other great towns; capital was absorbed by the mad speculations in railway shares; and even Heaven's gift of an abundant harvest, by at once lowering the price of corn, helped to depress commerce. Many banks stopped payment, and even the Bank of England seemed imperilled, saving itself only by adopting a bold line of policy advised by Government. At the same time, the Chartist movement was gathering the strength which was to expend itself in the futile demonstrations of 1848.

But as if it were not enough for every department of political or commercial life to be so seriously affected, there was now arising within the English National Church itself a singular movement, destined to affect the religious history of the land as powerfully, if not as beneficially, as did the Evangelical revival of the last century; and the National Kirk of Scotland, after long and stern contention on the crucial point of civil control in things spiritual, was ready for that rending in twain from which arose the Free Kirk; while other religious bodies were torn by the same keen spirit of strife, the same revolt against ancient order, as that which was distracting the world of politics. The bitterness of the disruption in Scotland is well-nigh exhausted, though the controversy enlisted at the time all the fervid power of a Chalmers; men honour the memory of the champions, while hoping to see the once sharp differences composed for ever. But the "Catholic Revival," initiated under the leadership of Newman, Pusey, and Keble, has proved to be no transient disturbance: and no figure has in relation to the Church history of the half-century the same portentous importance as that of John Henry Newman, whose powerful magnetism, as it attracted or repelled, drew men towards Romanism or drove them towards Rationalism, his logical art, made more impressive by the noble eloquence with which he sometimes adorned it, seeming to leave those who came under his spell no choice between the two extremes. When he finally decided on withdrawing himself from the Anglican and giving in his adhesion to the Roman communion, he set an example that

Anne E. Keeling

has not yet ceased to be imitated, to the incalculable damage of the English Establishment. Happily the massive Nonconformity of the country was hardly touched either by his influence or his example.

It is pleasant to turn from scenes of doubt and discord, of strife and sorrow, to that bright domestic life which was now vouchsafed to the Sovereign, as if in direct compensation for the storms that raved and beat outside her home—a home now brightened by the presence of five joyous, healthy children. It is a charming picture of the royal pair and of the manner of life in the palace—styled by one foreigner "the one really pleasant, comfortable English house, in which one feels at one's ease "—that is given us by the finely discerning Mendelssohn, invited by the Prince to "come and try his organ" before leaving England in 1842, on which occasion the Queen joined her husband and his guest at the instrument, enjoying and aiding in their musical performance, and singing, "quite faultlessly and with charming feeling and expression," a song written by the great master who was now paying a farewell visit, with nothing of ceremony in it, to English royalty. With a few touches Mendelssohn makes us see the delightful ease and comfort of this royal interior, the Queen gathering up the sheets of music strewn by the wind over the floor—the Prince cleverly managing the organ-stops so as to suit the master while he played—the mighty rocking-horse and the two birdcages beside the music-laden piano in the Queen's own sitting-room, beautiful with pictures and richly-bound books—the pretty difficulty about her finding some of Mendelssohn's own songs to sing to him, since her music was packed up and taken away to Claremont—her naive confession that she had been "so frightened" at singing before the master,—all are chronicled with not less zest and affection than the graceful gift of a valuable ring "as a remembrance" to the artist from the Queen, through Prince Albert. It is a much more pleasing impression that we thus obtain than can be given by details of State ceremonial and visits from other sovereigns. Of these last there was no lack, and the princely visitors were entertained with all due pomp and splendour; but neither on account of these costly entertainments nor on behalf of the royal children did the Sovereign ask the nation for so much as a shilling, the Civil List sufficing for every unlooked-for outlay, now that Prince Albert, by dint of persevering effort, had succeeded in putting the arrangements of the royal household on a satisfactory footing, sweeping away a vast number of time-honoured, thriftless expenses, and rendering a wise and generous economy possible.

Formerly the great officers of the Crown were charged with the oversight of the commonest domestic business of the palace. Being non-resident, these overseers did no over-seeing, and the actual servants were practically masterless. Hence arose numberless vexations and extravagant hind-rances. In 1843 this objectionable form of the division of labour was brought to an end, and one Master of the household who did his work replaced the many officials who, by a fiction of etiquette, had been formerly supposed to do everything while they did and could do nothing. The long-needed reform could not but be pleasing to the Queen, being quite in harmony with the upright principles that had always ruled her conduct, she having begun her reign by paying off the debts of her dead father—debts contracted not in her lifetime nor on her account, and which a spirit less purely honourable might therefore have declined to recognise.

Thanks to the Prince's able management, the royal pair found it in their power to purchase for themselves the estate of Osborne, in the Isle of Wight—a charming retreat all their own, which they could adorn for their delight with no thought of the thronging public; where the Prince could farm

Anne E. Keeling

and build and garden to his heart's content, and all could escape from the stately restraints of their burdensome rank, and from "the bitterness people create for themselves in London." Before very long they found for themselves that Highland holiday home of Balmoral which was to be so peculiarly dear, and in which Her Majesty—whose first visit to the *then* discontented Scotland was deemed quite a risky experiment—was so completely to win for herself the admiring love of her Scottish subjects.

At Balmoral Mr. Greville saw them some little time after their acquisition of the place, and witnesses to the "simplicity and ease" with which they lived, to the gay good humour that pervaded their circle—"the Queen running in and out of the house all day long, often going out alone, walking into the cottages, sitting down and chatting with the old women," the Prince free from trammels of etiquette, showing what native charm of manner and what high, cultivated intelligence were really his. The impression is identical with that conveyed by Her Majesty's published Journal of that Highland life; and, though lacking the many graceful details of that record, the testimony has its own value. Happy indeed was the Sovereign for whom the black cloud of those years showed such a silver lining! Other potentates were less happy, both as regarded their private blessings and their public fortunes.

It would be agreeable to English feelings, but not altogether consonant with historic truth, if we could leave unnoticed the scandalous attempts on the Queen's life which marked the earliest period of her reign and have been renewed in later days. The first attacks were by far of the most alarming character, but Her Majesty, whose escape on one occasion seemed due only to her husband's prompt action, never betrayed any agitation or alarm; and her dauntless bearing, and the care for others which she manifested by dispensing with the presence of her usual lady attendants when she anticipated one of these assaults, immensely increased the already high esteem in which her people held her. The first assailant, a half-crazy lad of low station named Oxford, was shut up in a lunatic asylum. For the second, a man named Francis, the same plea could not be urged; but the death-sentence he had incurred was commuted to transportation for life. Almost immediately a deformed lad called Bean followed the example of Francis. Her Majesty, who had been very earnest to save the life of the miserable beings attacking her, desired an alteration in the law as to such assaults; and their penalty was fixed at seven years' transportation, or imprisonment not exceeding three years, to which the court was empowered to add a moderate number of whippings—punishments having no heroic fascination about them, like that which for heated and shallow brains invested the hideous doom of "traitors." The expedient proved in a measure successful, none of the later assaults, discreditable as they are, betraying a really murderous intention. It has been remarked as a noteworthy circumstance that popular English monarchs have been more exposed to such dangers than others who were cordially disliked. It is not hatred that has prompted these assassins so much as imbecile vanity and the passion for notoriety, misleading an obscure coxcomb to think

"His glory would be great
According to *her* greatness whom he quenched."

Anne E. Keeling

CHAPTER III

FRANCE AND ENGLAND

It is necessary now to look at the relations of our Government with other nations, and in particular with France, whose fortunes just at this time had a clearly traceable effect on our own.

For several years the Court of England had been on terms of unprecedented cordiality with the French Court. The Queen had personally visited King Louis Philippe at the Chateau d'Eu—an event which we must go back as far as the days of Henry VIII to parallel—and had contracted a warm friendship for certain members of his family, in particular for the Queen, Marie Amelie, for the widowed Duchess of Orleans, a maternal cousin of Prince Albert, and for the perfect Louise, the truthful, unselfish second wife of Leopold, King of the Belgians, and daughter of the King of the French. It was a rude shock to all the warm feelings which our Queen, herself transparently honest, had learnt to cherish for her royal friends when the French King and his Minister, Guizot, entered into that fatal intrigue of theirs, "the Spanish marriages." Isabella, the young Queen of Spain, and her sister and heiress presumptive, Louisa, were yet unmarried at the time of the visit to the Chateau d'Eu; and about that time an undertaking was given by the French to the English Government that the Infanta Louisa should not marry a French prince until her sister, the actual Queen, "should be married and have children." The possible union of the crowns of France and Spain was known for a dream of French ambition, and was equally well known to be an object of dislike and dread to other European Powers. The engagement which the French King had now given seemed therefore well calculated to disarm suspicion and promote peace; but the one was reawakened and the other endangered when it became known that he had so used his power over the Spanish court as to procure that the royal sisters of Spain should be married on one day—Isabella, the Queen, to the most unfit and uncongenial of all the possible candidates for her hand; Louisa to King Louis Philippe's son, the Duke of Montpensier. The transaction on the face of it was far from respectable, since the credit and happiness of the young Spanish Queen seemed to have hardly entered into the consideration of those who arranged for her the *mariage de convenance* into which she was led blindfold; but when regarded as a violation of good faith it was additionally displeasing. Queen Victoria, to whom the scheme was imparted only when it was ripe for execution, through her personal friend Louise, Queen of the Belgians, replied to the communication in a tone of earnest, dignified remonstrance; but apparently the King was now too thoroughly committed to his scheme to be deterred by any reasoning or reproaches, and the tragical farce was played out. It had no good results for France; England was chilled and alienated, but the Spanish crown never devolved on the Duchess of Montpensier. Within two little years from her marriage that princess and all the French royal family fled from France, so hastily that they had scarcely money enough to provide for their journey, and appeared in England as fugitives, to be aided and protected by the Queen, who forgot all political resentment, and remembered only her personal regard for these fallen princes.

Anne E. Keeling

The overthrow of the Orleans dynasty in 1848 was a complete surprise, and men have never ceased to see something disgraceful in its amazing suddenness. Here was a great king, respected for wisdom and daring, and supposed to understand at every point the character of the land he ruled, his power appearing unshaken, while it was known to be backed with an army one hundred thousand strong. And almost without warning a whirlwind of insurrection against this solid power and this able ruler broke out, and in a few wild hours swept the whole fabric into chaos. Nothing caused more surprise at the moment than the extreme bitterness of animosity which the insurgents manifested towards the king's person, unless it were the tameness with which he submitted to his fate and the precipitancy of his flight. There was something rotten in the state of things, men said, which could thus dissolve, crushed like a swollen fungus by a casual foot. And indeed, whether with perfect justice or not, Louis Philippe's Administration had come to be deemed corrupt some time ere his fall. The free-spoken Parisians had openly flouted it as such: witness a mock advertisement placarded in the streets: "*A nettoyer, deux Chambres et une Cour*": "Two *Chambers* and a *Court* to clean." A French Government that had been crafty, but not crafty enough to conceal the fact, that was rather contemned for plotting than dreaded for unscrupulous energy, was already in peril. The still unsubdued revolutionary spirit, working under the smooth surface of French society, was the element which accomplished the destruction of this discredited Government.

The outbreak in France acted like a spark in a powder magazine; ere long great part of Europe was shaken by the second great revolutionary upheaval, when potentates seemed falling and ancient dynasties crumbling on all sides—a period of eager hope to many, followed by despair when the reaction set in, accompanied in too many places by repressive measures of pitiless severity. The contemptuous feeling with which many Englishmen were wont to view such Continental troubles is well embodied in the lines which Tennyson put into the mouth of one of his characters, speaking of France:

"Yonder, whiff! there comes a sudden heat,
The gravest citizen seems to lose his head,
The king is scared, the soldier will not fight.
The little boys begin to shoot and stab,
A kingdom topples over with a shriek
Like an old woman, and down rolls the world
In mock-heroics—
Revolts, republics, revolutions, most
No graver than a schoolboy's barring out;
Too comic for the solemn things they are,
Too solemn for the comic touches in them."

In this wild year 1848, which saw Revolution running riot on the Continent, England too had its share of troubles not less painfully ridiculous; the insurrection headed by Smith O'Brien, a chief of the "Young Ireland" party, coming to an inglorious end in the affray that took place at "the widow McCormick's cabbage-garden, Ballingarry," in the month of July; the greatly dreaded Chartist demonstration at Kennington Common on April 10th by its conspicuous failure having done much to damp the hopes and spirits of the party of disorder generally.

It would be easy now to laugh at the frustrated designs of the Chartist leaders and at the sort of panic they aroused in London: the vast procession, which was to have marched in military order to overawe Parliament, resolving itself into a confused rabble easily dispersed by the police, and the monster petition, that should have numbered six million signatures, transported piecemeal to the House, and there

Anne E. Keeling

found to have but two million names appended, many fictitious; the Chartist leader, completely cowed, thanking the Home Office for its lenient treatment; or, on the other hand, London and its peaceful inhabitants, distracted with wild rumours of combat and bloodshed, apprehending a repetition of Parisian madnesses, and unaware how thoroughly the Duke of Wellington, entrusted with the defence of the capital and its important buildings, had carried out all needful arrangements. The two hundred thousand special constables sworn in to aid in maintaining law and order on that day were visible enough, and had their utility in conveying a certain impression of safety; the troops whom the veteran commander held in readiness were kept out of sight till wanted. These rebellious spirits imagining themselves formidable and free, when caught in an invisible iron network—these terrified citizens, protected all unconsciously to themselves against the impotent foe whom they dreaded—might furnish food for mirth if we did not remember the real, deep, and widespread misery which found inarticulate but piteous expression in the movement now coming to confusion under the firm assertion of necessary authority. The disturbances must needs be quieted; but hitherto it has been the glory of our Victorian statesmen to have understood that the grievances which caused them must also be dealt with. Now that all which could be deemed wise and good in Chartist demands has been conceded, orderly and quietly, the name "Chartism" has utterly lost its dread significance.

No cruelly vindictive measures of reprisal followed the collapse of the agitation; none indeed were needed. The revolutionary epidemic, which had spread hitherward from France, found our body politic in too sound a condition, and could not fasten on it; and the subsequent convulsions which shook our great neighbour hardly called forth an answering thrill in England. The strange transactions of December 1851, by means of which Louis Napoleon Bonaparte,

Prince-President of the new French republic, succeeded in over-throwing that republic and replacing it by an empire of which he was the head, did indeed excite displeasure and distrust in many minds; and though it was believed that his high-handed proceedings had averted much disorder, the English Government was not prepared at once to accept all the proffered explanations of French diplomacy; but the then foreign Secretary, Lord Palmerston, by the rash proclamation of his individual approval, committed the Ministry of which he was one to a recognition of the *de facto* Monarch of France. This step was but the last of many instances in which Palmerston had acted without due reference to the premier's or the Sovereign's opinion—a course of conduct which had justly displeased the Queen, and had drawn from her grave and pointed remonstrances. The final transgression led to his resignation; but its effects on our relations with France remained.

Meanwhile the Emperor's consistent and probably sincere display of goodwill towards England, the apparent complacency with which the French nation acquiesced in his rule, and the outward prosperity accompanying it, did their natural work in conciliating approval, and in making men willing to forget the obscure and tortuous steps by which he had climbed to power. One day he and France were to pay for these things; but meanwhile he was a popular ruler, accepted and approved by the nation he governed, anxious for its prosperity, and earnest in keeping it friendly with Great Britain, which he had found a hospitable home in the days of his obscurity, which was again to offer an asylum to him in a day of utter disaster and overthrow, and where his life, chequered by vicissitudes stranger than any known to romance, was to come to a quiet close. It has been the singular fortune of Her Majesty to receive into the sacred shelter of her realm two dethroned monarchs, two fallen fortunes, two dynasties cast out from sovereign power, while

Anne E. Keeling

her own throne, "broad-based upon her people's will, and compassed by the inviolate sea," has stood firm and unshaken, even by a breath. And it has been her special honour to cherish with affection, even warmer in their adversity, the friends who had gained her regard when their prosperity seemed as bright and their great position as assured as her own. Visiting the Emperor Napoleon in his splendid capital, feted and welcomed by him and his Empress with every flattering form of honour that his ingenuity could devise or his power enable him to show, she did not forget the Orleans family and their calamities, but frankly urged on her host the injustice of the confiscations with which he had requited the supposed hostility of those princes, and endeavoured to persuade him to milder measures. She visited in his company the tomb of the lamented Duke of Orleans; and her first care on returning to England was to show some kindly attention to the discrowned royalties who were now her guests. In the same spirit, in after years, she extended a friendly hand to the exiled Empress Eugenie, escaping from new revolutionary perils to English safety, and altogether declined to consider her personal regard for the lady, whose attractions had deservedly gained it in brighter days, as being in any sense complicated with matters political. The resolute loyalty with which she at once maintained her private friendships and kept them entirely apart from her public action compelled toleration from the persons most inclined to take umbrage at it.

An instance of successful and courageous enterprise on Her Majesty's part may well close this brief notice of the internal and external convulsions which for a time shook, though they did not shatter, the peace of our realm. In the late summer of 1849 a royal visit to Ireland, now just reviving from its misery, was planned and carried out with complete success; the wild Irish enthusiasm blazed up into raptures of a loyal welcome, and the Sovereign, who played her part with all the graceful perfection that her compassionate heart and quick intelligence suggested, was delighted with the little tour, from which those who shared in it prophesied "permanent good" for Ireland. At least it had a healing, beneficial effect at the moment; and perhaps more could not have been reasonably hoped. Later royal visits to the sister isle have been less conspicuous, but all fairly successful.

Anne E. Keeling

CHAPTER IV

THE CRIMEAN WAR

The "Exhibition year," 1851, appears to our backward gaze almost like a short day of splendid summer interposed between two stormy seasons; but at the time men were more inclined to regard it as the first of a long series of halcyon days. Indeed, the unexampled number and success of the various efforts to redress injury and reform abuses, which had signalised the new reign, might almost justify those sanguine spirits, who now wrote and spoke as though wars and oppression were well on their way to the limbo of ancient barbarisms, and who looked to unfettered commerce as the peace-making civiliser, under whose influence the golden age—in more senses than one might revisit the earth.

We have already referred to certain of the new transforming forces whose action tended to heighten such hopes; there are two reforms as yet unnamed by us, distinguishing these early years, which are particularly significant; though one at least was stoutly opposed by a special class of reformers. We refer to the legislation dealing with mines and factories and those employed therein, with which is inseparably connected the venerable name of the late Lord Shaftesbury; and to the abolition of duelling in the army, secured by the untiring efforts of Prince Albert, who had enlisted on his side the immense influence of the Duke of Wellington.

That peculiar modern survival of the ancient trial by combat, the duel, was still blocking the way of English civilisation when Her Majesty assumed the sceptre. A palpable anachronism, it yet seemed impossible to make men act on their knowledge of its antiquated and barbarous character; legislation was fruitless of good against a practice consecrated by false sentiment and false ideas of honour; but when dislodged from its chief stronghold, the army, it became quickly discredited everywhere, with the happy result noted by a contemporary historian, that *now* "a duel in England would seem as absurd and barbarous as an ordeal by touch or a witch-burning." Militarism, that mischievous counterfeit of true soldierly spirit, could not thrive where the duel was discountenanced; and the friends of peace might rejoice with reason.

But those peaceful agitators, the sagacious, energetic Cobden and his allies, resented rather sharply the interference of the Lord Ashley of that day with the "natural laws" of the labour market—laws to whose operation some of the party attributed the cruelly excessive hours of work in factories, and the indiscriminate employment of all kinds of labour, even that of the merest infants. Undeterred by these objections, convinced that no law which sanctioned and promoted cruelty did so with true authority, Lord Ashley persisted in the struggle on which he had entered 1833; in 1842 he scored his first great success in the passing of an Act that put an end to the employment of women and children in mines and collieries; in 1844 the Government carried their Factories Act, which lessened and limited the hours of children's factory labour, and made other provisions for their benefit. It was not all that he had striven for, but it was much; he accepted the compromise, but did not slacken in his efforts still further to improve the condition of the

Anne E. Keeling

children. His career of steady benevolence far outstretched this early period of battle and endurance; but already his example and achievement were fruitful of good, and his fellow-labourers were numerous. Nothing succeeds like success: people had sneered at the mania for futile legislation that possessed the "humanity-monger" who so embarrassed party leaders with his crusade on behalf of mere mercy and justice; they now approved the practical philanthropist who had taken away a great reproach from his nation, and glorified the age in which they lived because of its special humaneness, while they exulted not less in the brightening prospects of the country. Sedition overcome, law and order triumphant, the throne standing firm, prosperity returning— all ministered to pride and hope.

In 1850 there had been some painful incidents; the death by an unhappy accident of Sir Robert Peel, and the turbulent excitement of what are known as the "No Popery" distur- bances, being the most notable: and of these again incomparably the most important was the untimely loss to the country of the great and honest statesman who might otherwise have rendered still more conspicuous services to the Sovereign and the empire. The sudden violent outburst of popular feeling, provoked by a piece of rash assumption on the part of the reigning Pope, was significant, indeed, as evidencing how little alteration the "Catholic revival" had worked in the temper of the nation at large; otherwise its historic importance is small. At the time, however, the current of agitation ran strongly, and swept into immediate oblivion an event which three years before would have had a European importance—the 'death of Louis Philippe, whose strangely chequered life came to an end in the old palace of Claremont, just before the "papal aggressions"—rash, impo- litic, and mischievous, as competent observers pronounced it, but powerless to injure English Protestantism—had thrown all the country into a ferment, which took some months to subside. We are told that Her Majesty, though naturally interested by this affair, was more alive to the quarter where the real peril lay than were some of her subjects; but in the universal distress caused by the death of Peel none joined more truly, none deplored that loss more deeply, than the Sovereign, who would willingly have shown her value for the true servant she had lost by conferring a peerage on his widow—an honour which Lady Peel, faithful to the wishes and sharing the feeling of her husband, felt it necessary to decline.

Amid these agitations, inferior far to many that had preceded them, the year 1850 ran out, and 1851 opened—the year in which Prince Albert's long-pursued project of a great International Exhibition of Arts and Industries was at last successfully carried out. The idea, as expounded by himself at a banquet given by the Lord Mayor, was large and noble. "It was to give the world a true test, a living picture, of the point of industrial development at which the whole of mankind had arrived, and a new starting-point from which all nations would be able to direct their further exertions." The magnificent success, unflawed by any vexatious or dangerous incident, with which the idea was carried out, had made it almost impossible for us to understand the opposition with which the plan was greeted, the ridicule that was heaped upon it, the foolish fears which it inspired; while the many similar Exhibitions in this and other countries that have followed and emulated, but never altogether equalled, the first, have made us somewhat oblivious of the fact that the scheme when first propounded was an absolute novelty. It was a fascination, a wonder, a delight; it aroused enthusiasm that will never be rekindled on a like occasion.

Paxton's fairy palace of glass and iron, erected in Hyde Park, and canopying in its glittering spaces the untouched, majestic elms of that national pleasure-ground as well as the varied

Anne E. Keeling

treasures of industrial and artistic achievement brought from every quarter of the globe, divided the charmed astonishment of foreign spectators with the absolute orderliness of the myriads who thronged it and crowded all its approaches on the great opening day. Perhaps on that day the Queen touched the summit of her rare happiness. It was the 1st of May—her own month—and the birthday of her youngest son, the godchild and namesake of the great Duke. She stood, the most justly popular and beloved of living monarchy, amid thousands of her rejoicing subjects, encompassed with loving friends and happy children, at the side of the beloved husband whose plan was now triumphantly realised; and she spoke the words which inaugurated that triumph and invited the world to gaze on it.

"The sight was magical," she says, "so vast, so glorious, so touching...God bless my dearest Albert! God bless my dearest country, which has shown itself so great to-day! One felt so grateful to the great God, Who seemed to pervade all and to bless all. The only event it in the slightest degree reminded me of was the coronation, but this day's festival was a thousand times superior. In fact, it is unique, and can bear no comparison, from its peculiar beauty and combination of such striking and different objects. I mean the slight resemblance only as to its solemnity; the enthusiasm and cheering, too, were much more touching, for in a church naturally all is silent."

The Exhibition remained open from the 1st of May to the 11th of October, continuing during all those months to attract many thousands of visitors. It had charmed the world by the splendid embodiment of peace and peaceful industries which it presented, and men willingly took this festival as a sign bespeaking a yet longer reign of world-tranquillity. It proved to be only a sort of rainbow, shining in the black front of approaching tempest. When 1854 opened, the third year from the Exhibition year, we were already committed to war with Russia; and the forty years' peace with Europe, finally won at Waterloo, was over and gone.

In the interval another great spirit had passed away. The Duke of Wellington died, very quietly and with little warning, at Walmer Castle, on the 14th of September, 1852, "full of years and honours." He was in his eighty-fourth year, and during the whole reign of Queen Victoria he had occupied such a position as no English subject had ever held before. At one time, before that reign began, his political action had made him extraordinarily unpopular, in despite of the splendid military services which no one could deny; now he was the very idol of the nation, and at the same time was treated with the utmost respect and reverent affection by the Sovereign—two distinctions how seldom either attained or merited by one person! But in Wellington's case there is no doubt that the popular adoration and the royal regard were worthily bestowed and well earned. He had never seemed stirred by the popular odium, he never seemed to prize the popular praise, which he received; it was not for praise that he had worked, but for simple duty; and his experience of the fickleness of public favour might make him something scornful of it. To the honours which his Sovereign delighted to shower on him—honours perhaps never before bestowed on a subject by a monarch—he *was* sensitive. The Queen to him was the noblest personification of the country whose good had ever been, not only the first, but the only object of his public action: and with this patriotic loyalty there mingled something of a personal feeling, more akin to romance in its paternal tenderness than seemed consistent with the granite-hewn strength and sternness of his general character. A thorough soldier, with a soldier's contempt for fine-spun diplomacy, he had been led into many a blunder when acting as a chief of party and of State; but his absolute single-minded honesty had more than redeemed such errors;

Anne E. Keeling

"integrity and uprightness had preserved him," and through him the land and its rulers, amid difficulties where the finest statecraft might have made shipwreck of all.

He had his human failings; yet the moral grandeur of his whole career cast such faults into the shade, and justified entirely the universal grief at his not untimely death. The Queen deplored him as "our immortal hero"—a servant of the Crown "devoted, loyal, and faithful" beyond all example; the nation endeavoured by a funeral of unprecedented sumptuousness to show its sense of loss; the poet laureate devoted to his memory a majestic Ode, hardly surpassed by any in the language for its stately, mournful music, and finely faithful in its characterisation of the dead hero—

"The man of long-enduring blood,
The statesman-warrior, moderate, resolute,
Whole in himself, a common good;...
...The man of amplest influence,
Yet clearest of ambitious crime,
Our greatest yet with least pretence,
Great in council and great in war,
Foremost captain of his time,
Rich in saving common-sense.
And, as the greatest only are.
In his simplicity sublime;...
Who never sold the truth to serve the hour,
Nor paltered with Eternal God for power;
Who let the turbid streams of rumour flow
Through either babbling world of high and low;
Whose life was work, whose language rife
With rugged maxims hewn from life;
Who never spoke against a foe;
Whose eighty winters freeze with one rebuke
All great self-seekers trampling on the right:
Truth-teller was our England's Alfred named;

Truth-lover was our English Duke;
Whatever record leap to light   He never shall be shamed."

When, within so short a period after Wellington's death, the nation once more found itself drawn into a European war, there were many whose regret for his removal was quickened into greater keenness. "Had we but the Duke to lead our armies!" was the common cry; but even *his* military genius might have found itself disastrously fettered, had he occupied the position which his ancient subordinate and comrade, Lord Raglan, was made to assume. It may be doubted if Wellington could have been induced to assume it.

Whether there ever would have been a Crimean war if no special friendliness had existed between France and England may be fair matter for speculation. The quarrel issuing in that war was indeed begun by France; but it would have been difficult for England to take no part in it. The apple of discord was supplied by a long-standing dispute between the Greek and Latin Churches as to the Holy Places situated in Palestine—a dispute in which France posed as the champion of the Latin and Russia of the Greek right to the guardianship of the various shrines. The claim of France was based on a treaty between Francis I and the then Sultan, and related to the Holy Places merely; the Russian claim, founded on a treaty between Turkey and Catherine II, was far wider, and embraced a protectorate over all Christians of the Greek Church in Turkey, and therefore over a great majority of the Sultan's European subjects. Such a construction of the treaty in question, however, had always been refused by England whenever Russia had stated it; and its assertion at this moment bore an ominous aspect in conjunction with the views which the reigning Czar Nicholas had made very plain to English statesmen, both when he visited England in 1844 and subsequently to that visit. To use his own well-known phrase, he regarded Turkey as "a sick man"—a

Anne E. Keeling

death-doomed man, indeed—and hoped to be the sick man's principal heir. He had confidently reckoned on English co-operation when the Turkish empire should at last be dismembered; he was now to find, not only that co-operation would be withheld, but that strong opposition would be offered to the execution of the plan, for which it had seemed that a favourable moment was presenting itself. The delusion under which he had acted was one that should have been dispelled by plain English speech long before; but now that he found it to be a delusion, he did not recede from his demands upon the Porte: he rather multiplied them. The upshot of all this was war, in spite of protracted diplomatic endeavours to the contrary; and into that war French and English went side by side. Once before they had done so, when Philip Augustus and Richard Coeur de Lion united their forces to wrest the Holy Places from the Saracens; that enterprise had been disgraced by particularly ugly scandals from which this was free; but in respect to glory of generalship, or permanent results secured, the Crimean campaign has little pre-eminence over the Fourth Crusade.

Recent disclosures, which have shown that Lord Aberdeen's Ministry was not rightly reproached with "drifting" idly and recklessly into this disastrous contest, have also helped to clear the English commander's memory from the slur of inefficiency so liberally flung on him at the time, while it has been shown that his action was seriously hampered by the French generals with whom he had to co-operate. From whatever cause, such glory as was gained in the Crimea belongs more to the rank and file of the allied armies than to those highest in command. The first success won on the heights of the Alma was not followed up; the Charge of the Six Hundred, which has made memorable for ever the Russian repulse at Balaklava, was a splendid mistake, valuable chiefly for the spirit-stirring example it has bequeathed to future generations of English soldiers, for its illustration of death-defying, disciplined courage; the great fight at Inkerman was only converted from a calamitous surprise into a victory by sheer obstinate valour, not by able strategy; and the operations that after Lord Raglan's death brought the unreasonably protracted siege of Sebastopol to a close did but evince afresh how grand were the soldierly qualities of both French and English, and how indifferently they were generalled.

If the allies came out of the conflict with no great glory, they had such satisfaction as could be derived from the severer losses and the discomfiture at all points of the foe. The disasters of the war had been fatal to the Czar Nicholas, who died on March 2nd, 1855, from pulmonary apoplexy—an attack to which he had laid himself open, it was said, in melancholy recklessness of his health. His was a striking personality, which had much more impressed English imaginations than that of Czar or Czarina since the time of Peter the Great; and the Queen herself had regarded the autocrat, whose great power made him so lonely, with an interest not untouched with compassion at the remote period when he had visited her Court and had talked with her statesmen about the imminent decay of Turkey. At that time the austere majesty of his aspect, seen amid the finer and softer lineaments of British courtiers, had been likened to the half-savage grandeur of an emperor of old Rome who should have been born a Thracian peasant. It proved that the contrast had gone much deeper than outward appearance, and that his views and principles had been as opposed to those of the English leaders, and as impossible of participation by such men as though he had been an imperfectly civilised contemporary of Constantine the Great. Since then he had succeeded in making himself more heartily hated, by the bulk of the English nation, than any sovereign since Napoleon I; for the war, into which the Government had entered reluctantly, was regarded by the people with great enthusiasm, and the foe was proportionately detested.

Many anticipated that the death of the Czar would herald in a triumphant peace; but in point of fact, peace was not signed until the March of 1856. Its terms satisfied the diplomatists both of France and England; they would probably have been less complacent could they have foreseen the day when this hard-won treaty would be torn up by the Power they seemed to be binding hand and foot with sworn obligations of perdurable toughness; least of all would that foresight have been agreeable to Lord Palmerston, Premier of England when the peace was signed, and quite at one with the mass of the people of England in their deep dislike and distrust of Russia and its rulers.

The political advantages which can be clearly traced to this war are not many. Privateers are no longer allowed to prey on the commerce of belligerent nations, and neutral commerce in all articles not contraband of war must be respected, while no blockade must be regarded unless efficiently and thoroughly maintained. Such were the principles with which the plenipotentiaries who signed the Treaty of Paris in 1856 enriched the code of international law; and these principles, which are in force still, alone remain of the advantages supposed to have been secured by all the misery and all the expenditure of the Crimean enterprise.

But other benefits, not of a political nature, arose out of the hideous mismanagement which had disgraced the earlier stages of the war. It is a very lamentable fact that of the 24,000 good Englishmen who left their bones in the Crimea, scarce 5,000 had fallen in fair fight or died of wounds received therein. Bad and deficient food, insufficient shelter and clothing, utter disorganisation and confusion in the hospital department, accounted for the rest. These evils, when exposed in the English newspapers, called forth a cry of shame and wrath from all the nation, and stirred noble men and women into the endeavour to mitigate at least the sufferings of the unhappy wounded. Miss Florence Nightingale, the daughter of a wealthy English gentleman, was known to take a deep and well-informed interest in hospital management; and this lady was induced to superintend personally the nursing of the wounded in our military hospitals in the East. Entrusted with plenary powers over the nurses, and accompanied by a trained staff of lady assistants, she went out to wrestle with and overcome the crying evils which too truly existed, and which were the despair of the army doctors. Her success in this noble work, magnificently complete as it was, did indeed "multiply the good," as Sidney Herbert had foretold: we may hope it will continue so to multiply it "to all time." The horrors of war have been mitigated to an incalculable extent by the exertions of the noble men and women who, following in the path first trodden by the Crimean heroines, formed the Geneva Convention, and have borne the Red Cross, its most sacred badge, on many a bloody field, in many a scene of terrible suffering—suffering touched with gleams of human pity and human gratitude; for the courageous tenderness of many a soft-handed and lion-hearted nursing sister, since the days of Florence Nightingale, has aroused the same half-adoring thankfulness which made helpless soldiers turn to kiss that lady's shadow, thrown by her lamp on the hospital wall.

The horrors thus mitigated have become more than ever repugnant to the educated perception of Christendom, because of the merciful devotion which, ever toiling to lessen them, keeps them before the world's eye. In every great war that has shaken the civilised world since the strife in the Crimea broke out, the ambulance, its patients, its attendants, have always been in the foreground of the picture. Never have the inseparable miseries of warfare been so well understood and so widely realised, thanks in part to

Anne E. Keeling

that new literary force of the Victorian age, the *war correspondent*, and chiefly, perhaps, to the new position henceforth assumed by the military medical and hospital service. To the same source we may fairly attribute the great improvements wrought in the whole conduct of that distinctively Christian charity, unknown to heathenism, the hospital system: the opening of a new field of usefulness to educated and devoted women of good position, as nurses in hospitals and out; and the vast increase of public interest in and public support of such agencies. Even the Female Medical Mission, now rising into such importance in the jealous lands of the East, may be traced not very indirectly to the same cause.

The Queen, whose enthusiasm for her beloved army and navy was very earnest, and frankly shown, who had suffered with their sufferings and exulted in their exploits, followed with a keen, personal, unfaltering interest the efforts made for their relief. "Tell these poor, noble wounded and sick men that *no one* takes a warmer interest, or feels more for their sufferings, or admires their courage and heroism more than their Queen. So does the Prince," was the impulsive, heart-warm message which Her Majesty sent for transmission through Miss Nightingale to her soldier-patients. Her deeds proved that these words were words of truth. Not content with subscribing largely to the fund raised on behalf of those left orphaned and widowed by the war, she took part in the work of providing fitting clothing for the men exposed to all the terrors of a Russian winter; and her daughters, enlisted to aid in this pious work, began that career of beneficence which two of them were to pursue afterwards to such good purpose, amid the ravages of wars whose colossal awfulness dwarfed the Crimean campaign in the memories of men.

Many of the injured being invalided home while the war was

in progress, Her Majesty embraced the opportunity to testify her sympathy and admiration, giving to them in public with her own hands the medals for service rendered at Alma, at Balaklava, and at Inkerman. It would not be easy to say whether the Sovereign or the soldiers were more deeply moved on this occasion. Conspicuous among the maimed and feeble heroes was the gallant young Sir Thomas Troubridge, who, lamed in both feet by a Russian shot at Inkerman, had remained at his post, giving his orders, while the fight endured, since there was none to fill his place. He appeared now, crippled for life, but declared himself "amply repaid for everything," while the Queen decorated him, and told him he should be one of her aides-de-camp. Her own high courage and resolute sense of duty moved her with special sympathy for heroism like this; and she obeyed the natural dictates of her heart in conspicuously rewarding it. With a similar impulse, on the return of the army, she made a welcoming visit to the sick and wounded at Chatham, and testified the liveliest appreciation of the humane services of Miss Nightingale, to whom a jewel specially designed by the Prince was presented, in grateful recognition of her inestimable work. The new decoration of the Victoria Cross, given "for valour" conspicuously shown in deeds of self-devotion in war time, further proved how keenly the Queen and her consort appreciated soldierly virtue. It was the Prince who first proposed that such a badge of merit should be introduced, the Queen who warmly accepted the idea, and in person bestowed the Cross on its first wearers, thereby giving it an unpurchasable value.

Anne E. Keeling

CHAPTER V

INDIA

Lord Aberdeen, who did not hope very great things from the war which had initiated during his Ministry, had yet deemed it possible that Eastern Europe might reap from it the benefit of a quarter of a century's peace. He was curiously near the mark in this estimate; but neither he nor any other English statesman was unwary enough to risk such a prophecy as to the general tranquillity of the Continent. In fact, the peace of Europe, broken in 1853, has been unstable enough ever since, and from time to time tremendous wars have shaken it. Into none of these, however, has Great Britain been again entrapped, though the sympathies of its people have often been warmly enlisted on this side and that. A war with China, which began in 1857, and cannot be said to have ended till 1860, though in the interim a treaty was signed which secured just a year's cessation of hostilities, was the most important undertaking in which the allied forces of France and England took part after the Crimea. In this war the allies were victorious, as at that date any European Power was tolerably certain to be in a serious contest with China. The closing act of the conflict—the destruction of the Summer Palace at Pekin, in retaliation for the treacherous murder of several French and English prisoners of distinction—was severely blamed at the time, but defended on the ground that only in this way could any effectual punishment of the offence be obtained. That act of vengeance and the war which it closed have an interest of their own in connection with the late General Gordon, who now entered on that course of extraordinary achievement which lacks a parallel in this century, and which began, in the interests of Chinese civilisation, shortly after he had taken a subordinate officer's part in the work of destruction at Pekin.

From this date England did not commit itself to any of the singular series of enterprises which our good ally, the French Emperor, set on foot. A feeling of distrust towards that potentate was invading the minds of the very Englishmen who had most cordially hailed his successes and met his advances. "The Emperor's mind is as full of schemes as a warren is full of rabbits, and, like rabbits, his schemes go to ground for the moment to avoid notice or antagonism," were the strong words of Lord Palmerston in a confidential letter of 1860; and when he could thus think and write, small wonder if calmer and more unprejudiced minds saw need for standing on their guard. Amid all the flattering demonstrations of friendship of which the French court had been lavish, and which had been gracefully reciprocated by English royalty, the Prince Consort had retained an undisturbed perception of much that was not quite satisfactory in the qualifications of the despotic chief of the French State for his difficult post. Thus it is without surprise that we find the Queen writing in 1859, as to a plan suggested by the Emperor: "The whole scheme is the often-attempted one, that England should take the chestnuts from the fire, and assume the responsibility of making proposals which, if they lead to war, we should be in honour bound to support by arms." The Emperor had once said of Louis Philippe, that he had fallen "because he was not sincere with England"; it looked now as though he were steering full on the same rock, for his own

Anne E. Keeling

sincerity was flawed by dangerous reservations.

England remained an interested spectator, but a spectator only, while the French ruler played that curiously calculated game of his, which did so much towards insuring the independence of Italy and its consolidation into one free monarchy. It was no disinterested game, as the cession of Nice and Savoy to France by Piedmont would alone have proved. It was daring to the point of rashness; for as a French general of high rank said, there needed but the slightest check to the French arms, and "it was all up with the dynasty!" Yet the "idea" which furnished the professed motive for the Emperor's warlike action was one dear to English sympathies, and many an English heart rejoiced in the solid good secured for Italy, though without our national co-operation. There was a proud compensating satisfaction in the knowledge that, when a crisis of unexampled and terrible importance had come in our own affairs, England had perforce dealt with it single-handed and with supreme success.

Those who can remember the fearful summer of 1857 can hardly recall its wild events without some recurrence of the thrill of horror that ran through the land, as week after week the Indian news of mutiny and massacre reached us. It was a surprise to the country at large, more than to the authorities, who were informed already that a spirit of disaffection had been at work among our native troops in Bengal, and that there was good reason to believe in the existence of a conspiracy for sapping the allegiance of these troops. Later events have left little doubt that such a conspiracy did exist, and that its aim was the total subversion of British power. Our advance in Hindostan had been rapid, the changes following on it many, and not always such as the Oriental mind could understand or approve. Early in the reign, in 1847, an energetic Governor-General, Lord Dalhousie, went out to India, who introduced railways, telegraphs, and cheap postage, set on foot a system of native education, and vigorously fought the ancient iniquities of suttee, thuggee, and child-murder. Perhaps his aggressive energy worked too fast, too fierily; perhaps his peremptory reforms, not less than his high-handed annexations of the Punjaub, Oude, and other native States, awakened suspicion in the mind of the Hindoo, bound as he was by the immemorial fetters of caste, and dreading with a shuddering horror innovations that might interfere with its distinctions; for to lose caste was to be outlawed among men and accursed in the sight of God.

Lord Canning, the successor of Lord Dalhousie, entered on his governor-generalship at a moment full of "unsuspected peril"; for the disaffected in Hindostan had so misread the signs of the times as to believe that England's sun was stooping towards its setting, and that the hour had come in which a successful blow could be struck, against the foreign domination of a people alien in faith as in blood from Mohammedan and Buddhist and Brahmin, and apt to treat all alike with the scorn of superiority. A trivial incident, which was held no trifle by the distrustful Sepoys, proved to be the spark that kindled a vast explosion. The cartridges supplied for use with the Enfield rifle, introduced into India in 1856, were greased; and the end would have to be bitten off when the cartridge was used. A report was busily circulated among the troops that the grease used was cow's fat and hog's lard, and that these substances were employed in pursuance of a deep-laid design to deprive every soldier of his caste by compelling him to taste these defiling things. Such compulsion would hardly have been less odious to a Mussulman than to a Hindoo; for swineflesh is abominable to the one, and the cow a sacred animal to the other. Whoever devised this falsehood intended to imply a subtle intention on the part of England to overthrow the native religions, which it was hoped the maddened soldiery would rise to resist. The

Anne E. Keeling

mischief worked as was desired. In vain the obnoxious cartridges were withdrawn from use; in vain the Governor-General issued a proclamation warning the army of Bengal against the falsehoods that were being circulated. Mysterious signals, little cakes of unleavened bread called *chupatties*, were being distributed, as the spring of 1857 went on, throughout the native villages under British rule, doing the office of the *Fiery Cross* among the Scotch Highlanders of an earlier day; and in May the great Mutiny broke out.

Some of the Bengal cavalry at Meerut had been imprisoned for refusing to use their cartridges; their comrades rose in rebellion, fired on their officers, released the prisoners, and murdered some Europeans. The British troops rallied and repulsed the mutineers, who fled to Delhi, unhappily reached it in safety, and required and obtained the protection of the feeble old King, the last of the Moguls, there residing. Him they proclaimed their Emperor, and avowed the intention of restoring his dynasty to its ancient supremacy. The native troops in the city and its environs at once prepared to join them; and thus from a mere mutiny, such as had occurred once and again before, the rising assumed the character of a vast revolutionary war. For a moment it seemed that our hard-won supremacy in the East was disappearing in a sea of blood. The foe were numerous, fanatical, and ruthless; we ourselves had trained and disciplined them for war; the sympathies of their countrymen were very largely with them. Yet, with incredible effort and heroism more than mortal, the small and scattered forces of England again snatched the mastery from the hands of the overwhelming numbers arrayed against them.

One name has obtained an immortality of infamy in connection with this struggle—that of the Nana Sahib, who by his hideous treachery at Cawnpore took revenge on confiding Englishmen and women for certain wrongs inflicted on him in regard to the inheritance of his adopted father by the last Governor-General. But many other names have been crowned with deathless honour, the just reward of unsurpassed achievement, of supreme fidelity and valour, at a crisis under which feeble natures would have fainted and fallen. Of these are Lord Canning himself, the noble brothers John and Henry Lawrence, the Generals Havelock, Outram, and Campbell, and others whom space forbids us even to name.

The Governor-General remained calm, resolute, and intrepid amidst the panic and the rage which shook Calcutta when the first appalling news of the Mutiny broke upon it. He disdained the cruel counsels of fear, and steadily refused to confound the innocent with the guilty among the natives; but he knew where to strike, and when, and how. On his own responsibility he stayed the British troops on their way to the scene of war in China, and made them serve the graver, more immediate need of India, doing it with the concurrence of Lord Elgin, the envoy responsible for the Chinese business; and he poured his forces on Delhi, the heart of the insurrection, resolving to make an end of it there before ever reinforcement direct from England could come. After a difficult and terrible siege, the place was carried by storm on September 20th, 1857—an achievement that cost many noble lives, and chief among them that of the gallant Nicholson, a soldier whose mind and character seem to have made on all who knew him an impression as of supernatural grandeur.

Five days later General Havelock and his little band of heroes—some one thousand Englishmen who had marched with him from Allahabad, recaptured by Neill for England, and on to ghastly Cawnpore—arrived at Lucknow, and relieved the slender British force which since May had been holding the Residency against the fierce and ever-renewed

Anne E. Keeling

assaults of the thousands of rebels who poured themselves upon it. He came in time to save many a brave life that should yet do good service; but the noblest Englishman of them all, the gentle, dauntless, chivalrous Sir Henry Lawrence, Governor of Oude, had died from wounds inflicted by a rebel shell many weeks before, and lay buried in the stronghold for whose safe keeping he had continued to provide in the hour and article of death. His spirit, however, seemed yet to actuate the survivors. Havelock's march had been one succession of victories won against enormous odds, and half miraculous; but even he could work no miracle, and his troops might merely have shared a tragic fate with the long-tried defenders of Lucknow, but for the timely arrival of Sir Colin Campbell with five thousand men more, to relieve in his turn the relieving force and place all the Europeans in Lucknow in real safety. The news was received in England with a delight that was mingled with mourning for the heroic and saintly Havelock, who sank and died on November 24th. A soldier whose military genius had passed unrecognised and almost unemployed while men far his inferiors were high in command, he had so more than profited by the opportunity for doing good service when it came, that in a few months his name had become one of the dearest in every English home, a glory and a joy for ever. It is rarely that a career so obscured by adverse fortune through all its course blazes into such sunset splendour just at the last hour of life's day.

Those months which made the fame of Havelock had been filled with crime and horror. The first reports of Sepoy outrages which circulated in England were undoubtedly exaggerated, but enough remains of sickening truth as to the cruelties endured by English women and children at the hand of the mutineers to account for the fury which filled the breasts of their avenging countrymen, and seemed to lend them supernatural strength and courage, and, alas! in some instances, to merge that courage in ferocity. Delhi had been deeply guilty, when the mutineers seized it, in respect of inhuman outrage on the helpless non-combatants; but the story of Cawnpore is darker yet, and is still after all these years fresh in our memories. A peculiar blackness of iniquity clings about it. That show of amity with which the Nana Sahib responded to the summons of Sir Hugh Wheeler, the hard-pressed commanding officer in the city, only that he might act against him; those false promises by which the little garrison, unconquerable by any force, was beguiled to give itself up to mere butchery; the long captivity of the few scores of women and children who survived the general slaughter, only, after many dreary days of painful suspense, to be murdered in their prison-house as Havelock drew near the gates of Cawnpore: all these circumstances of especial horror made men regard their chief instigator rather as one of the lower fiends masquerading in human guise than as a fellow-creature moved by any motives common to men. It was perhaps well for the fair fame of Englishmen that the Nana never fell into their hands, but saved himself by flight before the soldiers of Havelock had looked into the slaughter-house all strewn with relics of his victims and grimly marked with signs of murder, or had gazed shuddering at the dreadful well choked up with the corpses of their countrywomen. It required more than common courage, justice, and humanity, to withstand the wild demand for mere indiscriminating revenge which these things called forth. Happily those highest in power did possess these rare qualities. Lord Canning earned for himself the nickname of "Clemency Canning" by his perfect resoluteness to hold the balance of justice even, and unweighted by the mad passion of the hour. Sir John (afterwards Lord) Lawrence, the Chief Commissioner of the Punjaub, who, with his able subordinates, had saved that province at the very outset, and thereby in truth saved India, was equally firm in mercy and in justice. The Queen herself, who had very early appreciated

Anne E. Keeling

the gravity of the situation and promoted to the extent of her power the speedy sending of aid and reinforcement from England, thoroughly endorsed the wise and clement policy of the Governor-General. Replying to a letter of Lord Canning's which deplored "the rabid and indiscriminate vindictiveness abroad," Her Majesty wrote these words, which we will give ourselves the pleasure to quote entire:—

"Lord Canning will easily believe how entirely the Queen shares his feelings of sorrow and indignation at the unchristian spirit, shown, alas! also to a great extent here by the public, towards Indians in general, and towards Sepoys *without discrimination!* It is, however, not likely to last, and comes from the horror produced by the unspeakable atrocities perpetrated against the innocent women and children, which make one's blood run cold and one's heart bleed! For the perpetrators of these awful horrors no punishment can be severe enough; and sad as it is, *stern* justice must be dealt out to all the guilty.

"But to the nation at large, to the peaceable inhabitants, to the many kind and friendly natives who have assisted us, sheltered the fugitive, and been faithful and true, there should be shown the greatest kindness. They should know that there is no hatred to a brown skin—none; but the greatest wish on their Queen's part to see them happy, contented, and flourishing."

These words well became the sovereign who, by serious and cogent argument, had succeeded in inducing her Ministers to strike strongly and quickly on the side of law and order, they having been at first inclined to adopt a "step-by-step" policy as to sending out aid, which would not have been very grateful to the hard-pressed authorities in India; while the Queen and the Prince shared Lord Canning's opinion, that "nothing but a long continued manifestation of England's might before the eyes of the whole Indian empire, evinced by the presence of such an English force as should make the thought of opposition hopeless, would re-establish confidence in her strength."

The necessary manifestation of strength was made; the reputation of England—so rudely shaken, not only in the opinion of ignorant Hindoos, but in that of her European rivals—was re-established fully, and indeed gained by the power she had shown to cope with an unparalleled emergency. The counsels of vengeance were set aside, in spite of the obloquy which for a time was heaped on the true wisdom which rejected them. We did not "dethrone Christ to set up Moloch"; had we been guilty of that sanguinary folly, England and India might yet be ruing that year's doing. On the contrary, certain changes which did ensue in direct consequence of the Mutiny were productive of undoubted good.

It was recognised that the "fiction of rule by a trading company" in India must now be swept away; one of the very earliest effects of the outbreak had been to open men's eyes to the weak and sore places of that system. In 1858 an "Act for the better Government of India" was passed, which transferred to Her Majesty all the territories formerly governed by the East India Company, and provided that all the powers it had once wielded should now be exercised in her name, and that its military and naval forces should henceforth be deemed her forces. The new Secretary of State for India, with an assistant council of fifteen members, was entrusted with the care of Indian interests here; the Viceroy, or Governor-General, also assisted by a council, was to be supreme in India itself. The first viceroy who represented the majesty of England to the Queen's Indian subjects was the statesman who had safely steered us through the imminent, deadly peril of the Mutiny, and whom right feeling and

Anne E. Keeling

sound policy alike designated as the only fit wearer of this honour. Under the new regime race and class prejudices have softened, education is spreading swiftly, native oppression is becoming more difficult, as improved communications bring the light of day into the remoter districts of the immense peninsula. The public mind of England has never quite relapsed into its former scornful indifference to the welfare of India; rather, that welfare has been regarded with much keener interest, and the nation has become increasingly alive to its duty with regard to that mighty dependency, now one in allegiance with ourselves. There was much of happy omen in the reception accorded by loyal Hindoos to the Queen's proclamation when it reached them in 1858. While the mass of the people gladly hailed the rule of the "Empress," by whom they believed the Company "had been hanged for great offences," there were individuals who were intelligent enough to recognise with delight that noble character of "humanity, mercy, and justice," which was impressed by the Queen's own agency on the proclamation issued in her name. We may say that the joy with which such persons accepted the new reign has been justified by events, and that the same great principles have continued to guide all Her Majesty's own action with regard to India, and also that of her ablest representatives there.

We may not leave out of account, in reckoning the loss and gain of that tremendous year, the extraordinary examples of heroism called forth by its trials, which have made our annals richer, and have set the ideal of English nobleness higher. The amazing achievements and the swiftly following death of the gallant Havelock did not indeed eclipse in men's minds the equal patriotism and success of his noble fellows, but the tragic completeness of his story and the antique grandeur of his character made him specially dear to his countrymen; and the fact that he was already in his grave while the Queen and Parliament were busy in assigning to him the honours and rewards which his sixty years of life had hitherto lacked, added something like remorse to the national feeling for him. But the heart of the people swelled high with a worthy pride as we dwelt on his name and those of the Lawrences, the Neills, the Outrams, the Campbells, and felt that all our heroes had not died with Wellington.

Other anxieties and misfortunes had not been lacking while the fate of British India still hung in the balance. The attitude of some European Powers, whom the breaking forth of the Mutiny had encouraged in the idea that England's power was waning, was full of menace, especially in view of what the Prince Consort justly called "our pitiable state of unpreparedness" for resisting attack. Prompted by him, the Queen caused close inquiry to be made into the state of our home defences and of the navy—the first step towards remedying the deficiencies therein existing. Also a "cold wave" seemed to be passing over the commercial community in England; the year 1857 being marked by very great financial depression, which affected more or less every department of our industries. In connection with this calamity, however, there was at least one hopeful feature: the very different temper which the working classes, then, as always, the greatest sufferers by such depression, manifested in the time of trial. They showed themselves patient and loyal, able to understand that their employers too had evils to endure and difficulties to surmount; they no longer held all who were their superiors in station for their natural enemies: a happy change, testifying to the good worked by the new, beneficent spirit of legislation and reform.

It is under the date of this year that we find Mr. Greville, on the authority of Lord Clarendon, thus describing the very thorough and "eminently useful" manner in which the Queen, assisted by the Prince, was exercising her high functions:—

Anne E. Keeling

"She held each Minister to the discharge of his duty and his responsibility to her, and constantly desired to be furnished with accurate and detailed information about all important matters, keeping a record of all the reports that were made to her, and constantly referring to them; *e.g.*, she would desire to know what the state of the navy was, and what ships were in readiness for active service, and generally the state of each, ordering returns to be submitted to her from all the arsenals and dockyards, and again, weeks or months afterwards, referring to these returns, and desiring to have everything relating to them explained and accounted for, and so throughout every department....This is what none of her predecessors ever did, and it is, in fact, the act of Prince Albert."

We turn from this picture of the Sovereign's habitual occupations to her public life, and we find it never more full of apparently absorbing excitements—splendid hospitalities exchanged with other Powers, especially with Imperial France, alternating with messages of encouragement, full of cordiality and grace, to her successful commander-in-chief in India, Sir Colin Campbell, with plans for the conspicuous rewarding of the Indian heroes at large, with public visits to various great English towns, and with preparations for the impending marriage of the Princess Royal; and we realise forcibly that even in those sunny days, when the Queen was surrounded with her unbroken family of nine blooming and promising children, and still had at her right hand the invaluable counsellor by whose aid England was governed with a wisdom and energy all but unprecedented, her position was so far from a sinecure that no subject who had his daily bread to gain by his wits could have worked much harder.

CHAPTER VI

THE BEGINNINGS OF SORROWS

IT has been the Queen's good fortune to see her own true-love match happily repeated in the marriages of her children. One would almost say that the conspicuous success of that union, the blessing that it brought with it to the nation, had set a new fashion to royalty. There is quite a romantic charm about the first marriage which broke the royal home-circle of England—that of the Queen's eldest child and namesake, Victoria, Princess Royal, with Prince Frederick William, eldest son of the then Prince of Prussia, whose exaltation to the imperial throne of Germany lay dimly and afar—if not altogether undreamed of by some prophetic spirits—in the future. The bride and bridegroom had first met, when the youth was but nineteen and the maiden only ten, at the great Peace Festival, the opening of the first Exhibition. Already the charming grace and rare intelligence of the Princess had attracted attention; and it is on record that at this early period some inkling of a possible attraction between the two had entered one observer's mind, who also notes that the young Prince, greatly interested by all he saw of free England and its rulers, was above all taken with the "perfect domestic happiness which he found pervading the heart, and core, and focus of the greatest empire in the world." Four years later the Prince was again visiting England, a guest of the royal

Anne E. Keeling

family in its Scottish retreat of Balmoral, where they had just been celebrating with beacon fires and Highland mirth and music the glad news of the fall of Sebastopol. He had the full consent of his own family for his wooing, but the parents of his lady would have had him keep silence at least till the fifteen-year-old maiden should be confirmed. The ease and unconstraint of that mountain home-life, however, were not very favourable to reserve and reticence; a spray of white heather, offered and received as the national emblem of good fortune, was made the flower symbol of something more, and words were spoken that effectually bound the two young hearts, though the formal betrothal was deferred until some time after the Princess, in the following March, had received the rite of Confirmation; and "the actual marriage," said the Prince Consort, "cannot be thought of till the seventeenth birthday is past." "The secret must be kept *tant bien que mal*," he had written, well knowing that it would be a good deal of an open secret.

The engagement was publicly announced in May, 1857, and though, when first rumoured, it had been coldly looked on by the English public, now it was accepted with great cordiality. The Prince was openly associated with the royal family; he and his future bride appeared as sponsors at the christening of our youngest Princess, Beatrice; he rode with the Prince Consort beside the Queen when she made the first distribution of the Victoria Cross, and was a prominent and heartily welcomed member of the royal group which visited the Art Treasures Exhibition of Manchester. The marriage, which was in preparation all through the grim days of 1857, was celebrated with due splendour on January 25th, 1858, and awakened a universal interest which was not even surpassed when, five years later, the heir to the throne was wedded. "Down to the humblest cottage," said the Prince Consort, "the marriage has been regarded as a family affair." And not only this splendid and entirely successful match, but every joy or woe that has befallen the highest family in the land, has been felt as "a family affair" by thousands of the lowly. This is the peculiar glory of the present reign.

Happy and auspicious as this marriage was, it was nevertheless the first interruption to the pure home bliss that hitherto had filled "the heart of the greatest empire in the world." The Princess Royal, with her "man's head and child's heart," had been the dear companion of the father whose fine qualities she inherited, and had largely shared in his great thoughts. Nor was she less dear to her mother, who had sedulously watched over the "darling flower," admiring and approving her "touching and delightful" filial worship of the Prince Consort, and who followed with longing affection every movement of the dear child now removed from her sheltering care, and making her own way and place in a new world. There she has indeed proved herself, as she pledged herself to do, "worthy to be her mother's child," following her parents in the path of true philanthropy and gentle human care for the suffering and the lowly. So far the ancient prophecy has been well fulfilled which promised good fortune to Prussia and its rulers when the heir of the reigning house should wed a princess from sea-girt Britain. But the wedding so propitious for Germany seemed almost the beginning of sorrows for English royalty. Other betrothals and marriages of the princes and princesses ensued; but the still lamented death of the Prince Consort intervened before one of those betrothals culminated in marriage.

Another event which may be called domestic belongs to the year following this marriage—the coming of age of the Prince of Wales, fixed, according to English use and wont, when the heir of the crown completes his eighteenth year. Every educational advantage that wisdom or tenderness could suggest had been secured for the Prince. We may note in passing that one of his instructors was the Rev. Charles

Anne E. Keeling

Kingsley, whom Prince Albert had engaged to deliver a series of lectures on history to his son. This honour, as well as that of his appointment as one of Her Majesty's chaplains, was largely due to royal recognition of the practical Christianity, so contagious in its fervour, which distinguished Mr. Kingsley, not less than his great gifts; of his eagerness "to help in lifting the great masses of the people out of the slough of ignorance and all its attendant suffering and vice"—an object peculiarly dear to the Queen and to the Prince, as had been consistently shown on every opportunity.

When the time came that the youth so carefully trained should be emancipated from parental control, it was announced to him by the Queen in a letter characterised by Mr. Greville or his informant as "one of the most admirable ever penned. She tells him," continues the diarist, "that he may have thought the rule they adopted for his education a severe one, but that his welfare was their only object; and well knowing to what seductions of flattery he would eventually be exposed, they wished to prepare and strengthen his mind against them; that he was now to consider himself his own master, and that they should never intrude any advice upon him, although always ready to give it him whenever he thought fit to seek it. It was a very long letter, all in that tone; and it seems to have made a profound impression on the Prince.... The effect it produced is a proof of the wisdom that dictated its composition."

We have chosen this as a true typical instance of the blended prudence and tenderness that have marked the relations between our Sovereign and her children. Aware what a power for good or evil the characters of those children must have on the fortunes of very many others, she and her husband sedulously surrounded them with every happy and healthy influence, never forgetting the supreme need of due employment for their energies. "Without a vocation," said the Prince Consort, "man is incapable of complete development and real happiness": his sons have all had their vocation.

It was the same period, marked by these domestic passages of mingled joy and sorrow, that became memorable in another way, through the various troublous incidents which gave an extraordinary impetus to our national Volunteer movement, which were not remotely connected with the War of Italian Independence, and for a short time overthrew the popular Ministry of Lord Palmerston, who was replaced in office by Lord Derby. The futile plot of Felice Orsini, an Italian exile and patriot, against the life of Louis Napoleon, provoked great anger among the Imperialists of France against England, the former asylum of Orsini. A series of violent addresses from the French army, denouncing Great Britain as a mere harbour of assassins, did but give a more exaggerated form to the representations of French diplomacy, urging the amendment of our law, which appeared incompetent to touch murderous conspirators within our borders so long as their plots regarded only foreign Powers. The tone of France was deemed insolent and threatening; Lord Palmerston, who, in apparent deference to it, introduced a rather inefficient measure against conspiracy to murder, fell at once to the nadir of unpopularity, and soon had no choice but to resign; and the Volunteer movement in England—which had been begun in 1852, owing to the sinister changes that then took place in the French Government—now at once assumed the much more important character it has never since lost. The immense popularity of this movement and its rapid spread formed a significant reply to the insensate calls for vengeance on England which had risen from the French army, and which seemed worthy of attention in view of the vast increase now made in the naval strength of France, and of other preparations indicating that the Emperor meditated a great military enterprise. That enterprise proved to be the war with Austria which did so much for Italy, and which some observers were disposed to connect with the plot of Orsini— a rough reminder to the Emperor, they said, that he was trifling with the cause of Italian unity, to which he was secretly pledged. But Englishmen were slow to believe in such designs on the part of the French ruler. "How should a despot set men free?" was their thought, interpreted for them vigorously enough by an anonymous poet of the day; and they enrolled themselves in great numbers for national defence. With this movement there might be some evils mixed, but its purely defensive and manly character entitles it on the whole to be reckoned among the better influences of the day.

Palmerston's discredit with his countrymen was of short duration, as was his exile from office; he was Premier again in the June of 1859, and was thenceforth "Prime Minister for life." His popularity, which had been for some time increasing, remained now quite unshaken until his death in 1865. Before Lord Derby's Government fell, however, a reform had been carried which could not but have been extremely grateful to Mr. Disraeli, then the Ministerial leader of the House of Commons. The last trace of the disabilities under which the Jews in England had laboured for many generations was now removed, and the Baron Lionel de Rothschild was able quietly to take his seat as one of the members for the City of London. The disabilities in question had never interfered with the ambition or the success of Mr. Disraeli, who at a very early age had become a member of the Christian Church. But his sympathies had never been alienated from the own people, with whom indeed he had always proudly identified himself by bold assertion of their manifold superiority. There are still, undoubtedly, persons in this country whose convictions lead them to think it anything but a wholesome change which has admitted among our legislators men, however able and worthy, who disclaim the name of *Christian*. But the change was brought about by the conviction, which has steadily deepened among us, that oppression of those of a different faith from our own, either by direct severities or by the withholding of civil rights, is a singularly poor weapon of conversion, and that the adversaries of Christianity are more likely to be conciliated by being dealt with in a Christlike spirit; further, that religious opinion may not be treated as a crime, without violation of God's justice. On the point as to the claim of *irreligious* opinion to similar consideration, the national feeling cannot be called equally unanimous. In the case of the English Jews, it may be said that the tolerant and equal conduct adopted towards them has been well requited; the ancient people of God are not here, as in lands where they are trampled and trodden down, an offence and a trouble, the cause of repeated violent disturbance and the object of a frenzied hate, always deeply hurtful to those who entertain it.

Other changes and other incidents that now occurred engrossed a greater share of the public attention than this measure of relief. The rapid march of events in Italy had been watched with eager interest, divided partly by certain ugly outbreaks of Turkish fanaticism in Syria, and by our proceedings in the Ionian islands, which finally resulted in the quiet transfer of those isles to the kingdom of Greece. The commercial treaty with France effected, through the agency of Mr. Cobden, on Free Trade lines, and Mr. Gladstone's memorable success in carrying the repeal of the paper duty, and thereby immensely facilitating journalistic enterprise, were hailed with great delight as beneficial and truly progressive measures. But events of a more gigantic character now took place, which at the moment affected our prosperity more directly than any fiscal reform, and appealed more powerfully to us than the savagery of our Turkish *proteges* or even than the union of Italy under Victor

Anne E. Keeling

Emmanuel into one free and friendly State. The long-smouldering dissensions between the Northern and Southern States of the American Union at last broke into flame, and war was declared between them, in 1861.

The burning question of slavery was undoubtedly at the bottom of this contest, which has been truly described as a struggle for life between the "peculiar institution" and the principles of modern society. The nobler and more enthusiastic spirits in the Northern States beheld in it a strife between Michael and Satan, the Spirit of Darkness hurling himself against the Spirit of Light in a vain and presumptuous hope to overpower him; and their irritation was great when an eminent English man of letters was found describing it scornfully as "the burning of a dirty chimney," and when English opinion, speaking through very many journalists and public men, appeared half hostile to the Northern cause. Indeed, it might have been thought that opinion in England—England, which at a great cost had freed its own slaves, and which had never ceased by word and deed to attack slavery and the slave-trade—would not have faltered for a moment as to the party it would favour, but would have declared itself massively against the slave-holding South. But the contest at its outset was made to wear so doubtful an aspect that it was possible, unhappily possible, for many Englishmen of distinction to close their eyes to the great evils championed by the Southern troops. The war was not avowedly made by the North for the suppression of slavery, but to prevent the Southern States from withdrawing themselves from the Union: the Southerners on their side claimed a constitutional right so to withdraw if it pleased them, and denounced the attempt to retain them forcibly as a tyranny.

This false colouring at first given to the contest had mischievous results. English feeling was embittered by the great distress in our manufacturing districts, directly caused up the action of the Northern States in blockading the Southern ports, and thus cutting off our supply of raw material in the shape of cotton. On its side the North, which had calculated securely on English sympathy and respect, and was profoundly irritated by the many displays of a contrary feeling; and the exasperation on both sides more than once reached a point which made war appear almost inevitable—a war above all others to be deprecated. First came the affair of the *Trent*—the English mail-steamer from which two Southern envoys were carried off by an American naval commander, in contempt of the protection of the British flag. The action was technically illegal, and on the demand of the English Government its illegality was acknowledged, and the captives were restored; but the warlike and threatening tone of England on this occasion was bitterly resented at the North, and this resentment was greatly increased when it became known that various armed cruisers, in particular the notorious *Alabama*, designed to prey on the Northern commerce, were being built and fitted by English shipbuilders in English dockyards under the direction of the Southern foe, while the English Government could not decide if it were legally competent for Her Majesty's Ministers to interfere and detain such vessels. The tardy action at last taken just prevented the breaking out of hostilities. Out of these unfortunate transactions a certain good was to ensue at a date not far distant, when, after the restoration of peace, America and England, disputing as to the compensation due from one to the other for injuries sustained in this matter, gave to the world the great example of two nations submitting a point so grave to peaceful arbitration, instead of calling in the sword to make an end of it—an example more nearly pointing to the possible extinction of war than any other event of the world's history.

Yet another hopeful feature may be noted in connection with

Anne E. Keeling

this time of trouble. While the Secession war lasted, "the cotton famine" had full sway in Lancashire; unwonted and unwelcome light and stillness replaced the dun clouds of smoke and the busy hum that used to tell of fruitful, well-paid industry; and the patient people, haggard and pale but sadly submissive, were kept, and just kept, from starving by the incessant charitable effort of their countrymen. Never had the attitude of the suffering working classes shown such genuine nobility; they understood that the calamity which lay heavy on them was not brought about by the careless and selfish tyranny of their worldly superiors, but came in the order of God's providence; and their conduct at this crisis proved that an immense advance had been made in kindliness between class and class, and in true intelligence and appreciation of the difficulties proper to each. It was significant of this new temper that when at last peace returned, bringing some gleam of returning prosperity, the workers, who greeted with joyful tears the first bales of cotton that arrived, fell on their knees around the hopeful things and sang hymns of thanksgiving to the Author of all good.

Such were the fruits of that new policy of care and consideration for the toilers and the lowly which had increasingly marked the new epoch, and which had been sedulously promoted by the Queen, in association with her large-thoughted and well-judging husband.

It was in the midst of the troubles which we have just attempted to recall that a new and greater calamity came upon us, affecting the royal family indeed with the sharpest distress, but hardly less felt, even at the moment, by the nation.

The year 1861 had already been darkened for Her Majesty by the death in the month of March, of her mother, the

Duchess of Kent, to whose wise guardianship of the Queen's youth the nation owed so much, and who had ever commanded the faithful affection of this her youngest but greatest child, and of all her descendants. This death was the first stroke of real personal calamity to the Queen; it was destined to be followed by another bereavement, even severer in its nature, before the year had closed. The Prince Consort's health, though generally good, was not robust, and signs had not been wanting that his incessant toils were beginning to tell upon him. There had been illnesses, transitory indeed, but too significant of "overwork of brain and body." In addition to personal griefs, such as the death of the Duchess of Kent and of a beloved young Coburg prince and kinsman, the King of Portugal, which had been severely felt, there were the unhappy complications arising out of "the affair of the *Trent*," which the Prince's statesmanlike wisdom had helped to bring to a peaceful and honourable conclusion. That wisdom, unhappily, was no longer at the service of England when a series of negligences and ignorances on the part of England's statesmen had landed us in the *Alabama* difficulty.

All these agitations had told upon a frame which was rather harmoniously and finely than vigorously constituted. "If I had an illness," he had been known to say, "I am sure I should not struggle for life. I have no tenacity of life." And in the November of 1861 an illness came against which he was not able to struggle, but which took all the country by surprise when, on December 14th, it terminated in death. Very many had hardly been aware that there was danger until the midnight tolling of the great bell of St. Paul's startled men with an instant foreboding of disaster. *What* disaster it was that was thus knelled forth they knew not, and could hardly believe the tidings when given in articulate words.

Anne E. Keeling

At first it had been said, the Prince had a feverish cold; presently the bulletin announced "fever, unattended with unfavourable symptoms." It was gastric fever, and before long there *were* unfavourable symptoms—pallid changes in the aspect, hurried breathing, wandering senses—all noted with heart-breaking anxiety by the loving nurses, the Queen and Princess Alice—the daughter so tender and beloved, the "dear little wife," the "good little wife," whose ministerings were so comfortable to the sufferer overwearied with the great burden of life. He was released from it at ten minutes to eleven on the night of Saturday, December 14th; and there fell on her to whom his last conscious look had been turned, his last caress given, a burden of woe almost unspeakable, and for which the heart of the nation throbbed with well-nigh unbearable sympathy. Seldom has the personal grief of a sovereign been so keenly shared by subjects. Indeed, they had cause to lament; the removal of the Prince Consort, just when his faculties seemed ripest and his influence most assured, left a blank in the councils of the nation which has never been filled up. "We have buried our *king*" said Mr. Disraeli, regretting profoundly this national loss; but for once the English people forgot the public deprivation in compassionating her who was left more conspicuously lonely, more heavily burdened, than even the poor bereaved colliers' wives in the North for whom *her* compassion was so quick and so sharply sympathetic. Something remorseful mingled then, and may mingle now, with the affection felt for this lost benefactor, who had not only been somewhat jealously eyed by certain classes on his first coming, but who had suffered much silently from misunderstanding and also from deliberate misrepresentation, and only by patient continuance in well-doing had at last won the favour which was his rightful due.

"That which we have we prize not to the worth
While we enjoy it; but being lacked and lost,

Why, then we rack the value, then we find
The virtue that possession would not show us
While it was ours."

A peculiar tenderness was ever after cherished for Princess Alice, who in this dark hour rose up to be her mother's comforter, endeavouring in every way possible to save her all trouble—"all communications from the Ministers and household passed through the Princess's hands to the Queen, then bowed down with grief.... It was the very intimate intercourse with the sorrowing Queen at that time which called forth in Princess Alice that keen interest and understanding in politics for which she was afterwards so distinguished. The gay, bright girl suddenly developed into a wise, far-seeing woman, living only for others."

This ministering angel in the house of mourning had been already betrothed, with her parents' full approval, to Prince Louis of Hesse; and to him she was married on July 1st, 1862, at Osborne, very quietly, as befitted the mournful circumstance of the royal family. Many a heartfelt wish for her happiness followed "England's England-loving daughter" to her foreign home, where she led a beautiful, useful life, treading in her father's footsteps, and continually cherished by the love of her mother; and the peculiarly touching manner of her death, a sort of martyrdom to sweet domestic affections, again stirred the heart of her own people to mournful admiration. A cottager's wife might have died as Princess Alice died, through breathing in the poison of diphtheria as she hung, a constant, loving nurse, over the pillows of her suffering husband and children. This beautiful *homeliness* that has marked the lives of our Sovereign and her children has been of inestimable value, raising simple human virtues to their proper pre-eminence before the eyes of the English people of to-day, who are very materially, if often unconsciously, swayed by the example set them in

Anne E. Keeling

high places.

In the May after Prince Consort's death the second International Exhibition was opened, amid sad memories of the first, so joyful in every way, and a certain sense of discouragement because the golden days of universal peace seemed farther off than ten years before.

"Is the goal so far away?
Far, how far no tongue can say;
Let us dream our dream to-day."

Far indeed it seemed, with the fratricidal contest raging in America, and shutting out all contributions to this World's Fair from the United States.

The Queen had betaken herself that May to her Highland home, whose joy seemed dead, and where her melancholy pleased itself in the erection of a memorial cairn to the Prince on Craig Lorigan, after she had returned from Princess Alice's wedding. But in May she had sent for Dr. Norman Macleod, who was not only distinguished as one of her own chaplains, but was also a friend already endeared to the Prince and herself; and she found comfort in the counsels of that faithful minister and loyal man, who has left some slight record of her words. "She said she never shut her eyes to trials, but liked to look them in the face; she would never shrink from duty, but all was at present done mechanically; her highest ideas of purity and love were obtained from the Prince, and God could not be displeased with her love.... There was nothing morbid in her grief.... She said that the Prince always believed he was to die soon, and that he often told her that he had never any fear of death." It seemed that in this persuasion the Prince had made haste to live up to the duties of his difficult station to the very utmost, and "being made perfect in a short time fulfilled a long time [Footnote]."

[Footnote: Inscription on the cairn on Craig Lorigan.]

"The more I learn about the Prince Consort," continues Dr. Macleod, "the more I agree with what the Queen said to me about him: 'that he really did not seem to comprehend a selfish character, or what selfishness was.' And on whatever day his public life is revealed to the world, I feel certain this will be recognised."

The Queen, by revealing to the world, with a kind of holy boldness, what the Prince's public and private life was, has justified this confidence of her faithful friend.

Early in 1863, Dr. Macleod was led by the Queen into the mausoleum she had caused to be raised for her husband's last resting-place. Calm and quiet she stood and looked on the beautiful sculptured image of him she had lost: having "that within which passeth show," her grief was tranquil. "She is so true, so genuine, I wonder not at her sorrow; it but expresses the greatest loss that a sovereign and wife could sustain," said the deeply moved spectator.

An event was close at hand which was to mingle a little joy in the bitter cup so long pressed to our Sovereign's lips. The Prince of Wales had formed an attachment to the Princess Alexandra of Denmark, a singularly winning and lovely lady, whose popularity, ever since her sweet face first shone on the surging crowds that shouted her welcome into London, has seemed always at flood-tide. Faithful to her experience and convictions, the Queen smiled gladly on the marriage of affection between this gentle princess and the heir to the throne, and was present as a spectator, though still wearing her sombre weeds, at the splendid show of her son's wedding on March 10th, 1863. "Two things have struck me much," writes Dr. Macleod, from whose Journal we again quote: "one was the whole of the royal princesses weeping,

Anne E. Keeling

though concealing their tears with their bouquets, as they saw their brother, who was to them but their 'Bertie' and their dear father's son, standing alone waiting for his bride. The other was the Queen's expression as she raised her eyes to heaven while her husband's *Chorale* was sung. She seemed to be with him alone before the throne of God."

"No possible favour can the Queen grant me, or honour bestow," said the manly writer of these words, "beyond what the poor can give the poor—her friendship." It is rarely that one sitting amid "the fierce light that beats upon the throne" has been able to enjoy the simple bliss of true, disinterested friendship with those of kindred soul but inferior station. Such rare fortune, however, has been the Queen's; and it is worthy of note that her special regard has been won by persons distinguished not less by loftiness and purity of character than by mental power or personal charm. She has not escaped the frequent penalty of strong affection, that of being bereaved of its objects. She has outlived earlier and later friends alike—Lady Augusta Stanley and her husband, the beloved Dean of Westminster; the good and beautiful Duchess of Sutherland; the two eminent Scotchmen, Principal Tulloch and Dr. Macleod himself; and the Archbishop of Canterbury, Dr. Tait, with his charming wife. To these might be added, among the more eminent objects of her regard, the late poet laureate, who shared with Macaulay the once unique privilege of having been raised to the peerage more for transcendent ability than for any other motive—a distinction that never would have been so bestowed by our early Hanoverian kings, and which offers a marked contrast to the sort of patronage with which later sovereigns have distinguished the great writers of their time. A new spirit rules now; of this no better evidence could be given than this recently published testimony to the relations between Queen and poet: "Mrs. Tennyson told us that the poet laureate likes and admires the Queen personally very much, and enjoys conversation with her. Mrs. Tennyson generally goes too, and says the Queen's manner towards him is childlike and charming, and they both give their opinions freely, even when those differ from the Queen's, which she takes with perfect good humour, and is very animated herself [Footnote]."

[Footnote: "Anne Gilchrist: her Life and Writings." London: 1887.]

CHAPTER VII

CHANGES GOOD AND EVIL

With the death of Lord Palmerston in 1865, a sort of truce in the strife of parties, which his supremacy had secured, came to an end. That supremacy had been imperilled for a moment when the Government declined to make an armed intervention in the struggle between Denmark and the German Powers in 1864. Such an intervention would have been very popular with the English people, who could hardly know that "all Germany would rise as one man" to repel it if it were risked. But the English Premier's rare command of his audience in Parliament enabled him to overcome even this difficulty; and the gigantic series of contests on the Continent which resulted in the consolidation of the German empire, the complete liberation of Italy, the overthrow of Imperialism in France and of the temporal power of the Pope even in Rome itself, went on its way without our interference also, which would hardly have been the case had we intermeddled in the ill-understood contention between Denmark and its adversaries as to the Schleswig-Holstein succession.

That strange crime, the murder of President Lincoln, in America just when the long contest between North and South had ended and the cause of true freedom had triumphed, was actually fruitful of good as regarded this country and the United States. A cry of horror went up from all England at the news of that "most accursed assassination," which seemed at the moment to brand the losing cause, whose partisan was guilty of it, with the very mark of Cain. Expressions of sympathy with the outraged country and of admiring regret for its murdered head were lavished by every respectable organ of opinion; while the Queen, by writing in personal sympathy, as one widow to another, to the bereaved wife of Lincoln, made herself, as she has often done, the mouthpiece of her people's best feeling. Again and again has it been manifested that America and England are in more cordial relations with each other since the tremendous civil war than before it. It is no matter of statecraft, but a better understanding between two great English-speaking peoples, drawn into closer fellowship by far more easy communication than of old.

A little war with Ashantee, not too successful, a difficulty with Japan, some more serious troubles with New Zealand, exhaust the list of the warlike enterprises of England in the last years of Palmerston. In a year or two after his death we were engaged in a brief and entirely successful campaign against the barbaric King Theodore of Abyssinia, "a compound of savage virtue and more than savage ambition and cruelty," who, imagining himself wronged and slighted by England, had seized a number of British subjects, held them in hard captivity, and treated them with such capricious cruelty as made it very manifest that their lives were not worth an hour's purchase. It fell to the Ministry of Mr. Disraeli, Premier on the resignation of his colleague Lord Derby, who had displaced Earl Russell in that office, to bring this strange potentate to reason by force of arms. Under Sir Robert Napier's management the work was done with remarkable precision; no English life was lost; and but few of our soldiers were wounded; Magdala, the mountain eyrie of King Theodore, was stormed and destroyed, and the captives, having been surrendered under dread of the British arms, were restored to freedom and safety. The honour of our land, imperilled by the oppression of our subjects was triumphantly vindicated; other good was not achieved. Theodore, unwilling to survive defeat, was found dead by his own hand when Magdala was carried, and he was afterwards succeeded on the Abyssinian throne by a chief who had more than all his predecessor's vices and none of his virtues. For this well-managed campaign Sir Robert Napier was raised to the peerage as Lord Napier of Magdala. The swift success, the brilliant promptitude, of his achievement are almost painful to recall to-day, in face of another enterprise for the rescue of a British subject, conducted by a commander not less able and resolute, at the head of troops as daring and as enthusiastic, which was turned into a conspicuous failure by unhappy delayings on the part of the civil authorities, in the fatal winter of 1884-5.

Turning our eyes from foreign matters to the internal affairs of the United Kingdom, we see two great leaders, Mr. Disraeli and Mr. Gladstone—whose "long Parliamentary duel" had begun early in the fifties of this century—outbidding each other by turns for the public favour, and each in his different way ministering to the popular craving for reform. With Mr. Disraeli's first appearance as leader of the house of Commons, this rivalry entered on its most noticeable stage; it only really ceased with the life of the brilliant, versatile, and daring *litterateur* and statesman who died as Earl Beaconsfield, not very long after his last tenure of office expired in 1880. In 1867 Mr. Disraeli, as Leader of the Lower House, carried a measure for the reform of the franchise in England, and the year following similar measures with regard to Ireland and Scotland. In 1869 it was Mr. Gladstone's turn, and he introduced and carried two remarkable Bills—one for the disestablishment of the Irish

Church, and one for the amendment of land tenure in Ireland, the latter passing into law in August, 1870. It had long been felt as a bitter grievance by the mass of Irishmen that the Church established in their country should be one which did not command the allegiance of one-sixth of its people and though opinion in England was sharply divided as to the question of Irish disestablishment, the majority of Englishmen undoubtedly considered the grievance to be something more than a sentimental one, and deserving of removal. Another startling measure of reform was the abolition of purchase in the army, carried in the face of a reluctant House of Lords by means of a sudden exercise of royal prerogative under advice of the Government; the Premier announcing "that as the system of purchase was the creation of royal regulation, he had advised the Queen to take the decisive step of cancelling the royal warrant which made purchase legal"—a step which, however singular, was undoubtedly legal, as was proved by abundant evidence.

A measure which may not improbably prove to have affected the fortunes of this country more extensively than any of those already enumerated was the Education Bill introduced by Mr. Forster in 1870, and designed to secure public elementary education for even the humblest classes throughout England and Wales. Hitherto the teaching of the destitute poor had been largely left to private charity or piety, and in the crowded towns it had been much neglected, with the great exception of the work done in Ragged Schools—those gallant efforts made by unpaid Christian zeal to cope with the multitudinous ignorance and misery of our overgrown cities. It was very slowly that the national conscience was aroused to the peril and sin of allowing the masses to grow up in heathen ignorance; but at last the English State shook off its sluggish indifference to the instruction of its poor, and became as active as it had been supine. Mr. Forster's Bill is the measure which indicates this turning of the tide. We do not propose now to discuss the provisions of this Act, which were sharply canvassed at the time, and which certainly have not worked without friction; but we may say that the stimulus then given to educational activity, if judged by subsequent results, must be acknowledged to have been advantageous. The system of schools under the charge of various religious bodies, which existed before the Education Act, has not been superseded; that indeed would have been a deep misfortune, for it is more needed than ever; the masses of the population have been, to an appreciable extent, reached and instructed; and we shall not much err in connecting as cause and effect the wider instruction with the diminution of pauperism and crime which the statistics of recent years reveal.

The same member who honoured himself and benefited his country by this great effort to promote the advance of the "angel Knowledge" also introduced, in 1871, the Ballot Bill, designed to do away with all the violence and corruption that had long disgraced Parliamentary elections in this free land, and that showed no symptom of a tendency to reform themselves. The new system of secret voting which was now adopted has required, it is true, to be further purified by the recent Corrupt Practices Bill and its stringent provisions; but no one, whose memory is long enough to recall the tumultuous and discreditable scenes attendant on elections under the old system, will be inclined to deny that much that was flagrantly disgraceful as well as dishonest has been swept away by the reforming energy of our own day.

It is to the same period, made memorable by these internal reforms, that we have to refer the final settlement of the long-standing controversy between Great Britain and the United States as to the *Alabama* claims. We have already referred to these claims and the peaceful though very costly manner of their adjustment. That the award on the whole should go against us was not very grateful to the English people; but when the natural irritation of the hour had time to subside, the substantial justice of the decision was little disputed. While England was thus busied in strengthening her walls and making straight her ways, her great neighbour and rival was passing through a very furnace of misery. The colossal-seeming Empire, whose head was rather of strangely mingled Corinthian metal than of fine gold, and whose iron feet were mixed with miry clay, was tottering to its overthrow, and fell in the wild days of 1870 with a world-awakening crash. Again it was a dispute concerning the throne of Spain which precipitated the fall of a French sovereign. It would seem as if interference with the affairs of its Southern neighbour was ever to be ominous of evil to France. The first great Napoleon had had to rue such interference; it had been disastrous to Louis Philippe; now Louis Napoleon, making the candidature of Leopold of Hohenzollern for the Spanish crown a pretext for war with Prussia, forced on the strife which was to dethrone himself, to cast down his dynasty, and to despoil France of two fair provinces, Alsace and Lorraine, once taken from Germany, now reconquered for United Germany. With that strife, which resulted in the exaltation of the Prussian King, our Princess Royal's father-in-law, as German Emperor, England had absolutely nothing to do, except to pity the fallen and help the suffering as far as in her lay; but it awakened profoundest interest, especially while the long siege of Paris dragged on through the hard winter of 1870-71; hardly yet is the interest of the subject exhausted.

A certain fleeting effect was produced in England by the erection of a New Republic in France in place of the fallen Empire, while the family of the defeated ruler—rejected by his realm more for lack of success than for his bad government—escaped to the safety of this country from the angry hatred of their own. A few people here began to talk republicanism in public, and to commend the "logical superiority" of that mode of government, oblivious of the fact that practical Britain prefers a system, however illogical, that actually works well, to the most beautifully reasoned but untested paper theory. But the wild excesses of the Commune in Paris, outdoing in horror the sufferings of the siege, quickly produced the same effect here that was wrought in the last century by the French Reign of Terror, and English republicanism relapsed into the dormant state from which it had only just awakened. The dangerous illness that attacked the Prince of Wales in the last days of 1871, calling forth such keen anxiety throughout the land that it seemed as if thousands of families had a son lying in imminent peril of death, showed at once that the nation was yet loyal to the core. True prayers were everywhere offered up in sympathy with the mother, the sister, the wife, who watched at the bedside of the heir to the throne; and when, on the very anniversary of the Prince Consort's death, the life that had seemed ebbing away turned to flow upward again; a sort of sob of relief rose from the heart of the people, who rejoiced to be able, at a later day, to share with their Queen her solemn act of thanksgiving for mercy shown, as she went with her restored son, her son's wife, and her son's sons, to worship and give praise in the great cathedral of St. Paul's.

Princess Alice, who had shared and softened the grief of her mother ten years before, had been again at her side during all the protracted anxiety of this winter, and had helped to nurse her brother. The Princess's experience of nursing had been terribly increased during the awful wars, when she had been incessantly busied in hospital organisation and work, suffering from the sight of suffering as a sensitive nature must, but ever toiling to lighten it; and she had come with her children to recover a little strength in her mother's Highland home. Thus it was that she was found at Sandringham when her brother's illness declared itself, "fulfilling the same priceless offices" of affection as in her maiden days, and endearing herself the more to the English people, who grieved for her when, in the ensuing year, a mournful accident robbed her of one darling child, and who felt it like a personal domestic loss when in 1878 the beautiful life ended. Other royal marriages have from time to time awakened public interest, and one, celebrated between the Princess Louise and the Marquis of Lorne, heir of the dukedom of Argyll, had just preceded the illness of the Prince and was regarded with much more attention because no British subject since the days of George II's legislation as to royal alliances had been deemed worthy of such honour. But not even the more outwardly splendid match between the Queen's sailor son, Alfred, Duke of Edinburgh, and the daughter of the Czar Alexander, could eclipse in popularity the quiet marriage, overclouded with sorrow, and the tranquil, hard-working life of the good and gifted lady who was to die the martyr of her true motherly and wifely devotion.

From these glimpses of the joys and troubles affecting the household that is cherished in the heart of England, we return to the more stormy records of our public doings. A sort of link between the two exists in the long and very successful tour which the Prince of Wales, some time after his restoration to health, made of the vast Indian dominions of the crown. Extensive travels and wide acquaintance with the great world to which Britain is bound by a thousand ties have entered largely into the royal scheme of education for the future King. No princes of England in former days have seen so much of other lands as the sons of Queen Victoria; and this particular journey is understood to have had an excellent political effect.

Mr. Gladstone's five years' lease of power, which had been signalised by so many important changes, came to an end in

Anne E. Keeling

1874, just before the time when Sir Garnet Wolseley, sent to bring the savage King of Ashantee to reason, returned successful to England, having snatched a complete victory "out of the very jaws of approaching sun and fever" on the pestilent West Coast of Africa in the early days of 1874. The last Ministry of Mr. Disraeli, who now assumed office, was marked by several noticeable events: the proclamation of the Queen as "Empress of India," in formal definite recognition of the new relation between little England and the gigantic, many-peopled realm which through strange adventure has come directly under our Sovereign's sway; the Russo-Turkish war, following on the evil doings in Turkey known as the "Bulgarian atrocities," and terminating in a peace signed at Berlin, with which the English Premier, now known as Lord Beaconsfield, had very much to do; and the acquisition by England of the 176,000 shares in the Suez Canal originally held by the Khedive of Egypt—a transaction to which France, also largely interested in the Canal, was a consenting party. To this period belong the distressful Afghan and Zulu wars, the latter unhappily memorable by the tragic fate that befell the young son of Louis Napoleon, a volunteer serving with the English army. Deep sympathy was felt for his imperial mother, widowed since 1873, and now bereaved of her only child; and by none was her sorrow more keenly realised than by the Queen, who herself had to mourn the loss of the beloved Princess Alice, the first of her children to follow her father into the silent land. The death of the Prince Louis Napoleon at the hands of savage Zulus was severely felt by the still strong Bonapartism of France; but Englishmen, remembering the early melancholy death of the heir of the first Napoleon, were struck by the fatal coincidence, while they could honestly deplore the premature extinction of so much youth, gallantry, and hope-fulness, cast away in our own ill-starred quarrel.

An agitation distinctly humanitarian and domestic had been going on during the early years of this Ministry, which resulted in the passing of the Merchant Shipping Bill, intended to remedy the many wrongs to which our merchant seamen were subject, a measure almost entirely procured by the fervent human sympathy and resoluteness of one member of Parliament, Samuel Plimsoll; and other measures belonging to this period, and designed to benefit the toilers of the land principally, were initiated by the energy of the Home Secretary, Mr. Cross. But neither the imposing foreign action of Lord Beaconsfield's Government, nor the domestic improvements wrought during its period of power, could maintain it in public favour. There was great and growing distress in the country; depression of trade, severe winters, sunless summers, all produced suffering, and suffering discontent. An appeal to the country, made in the spring of 1880, shifted the Parliamentary majority from the Conservative to the Liberal side. Lord Beaconsfield resigned, and Mr. Gladstone returned to power.

The history of the Gladstone Ministry does not come well within the scope of this work. Certain very memorable events must be touched upon; there are dark chapters of our national story, stains and blots on our great name, which force themselves upon us. But to follow the Government through its years of struggle with the ever-growing bulk of Irish difficulty, and to track it through its various enactments designed still further to improve the condition of the English people, would require a small volume to itself. England still remembers the thrill, half fury, half anguish, which ran through her at the tidings that the new Chief Secretary for Ireland, charged with a message of peace and conciliation, had been stabbed to death within twenty-four hours of his landing on that unhappy shore. She cannot forego the deep instinctive feeling—so generally manifested at the time of Lincoln's murder—that the lawless spilling of life for any

Anne E. Keeling

cause dishonours and discredits that cause; nor have various subsequent efforts made to terrorise public opinion here been differently judged.

But it was a far more cruel shock that was inflicted through the series of ill-advised proceedings that brought about the great disaster of Khartoum. Before we deal with these, we must glance at the African and Afghan troubles, again breaking out and again quieted, the first by a peace with the Boers of the Transvaal that awakened violent discussion not yet at an end, and the second, after some successes of the British arms, by a judicious arrangement designed to secure the neutrality of Afghanistan, interposed by nature as a strong, all but insurmountable, barrier between India and Central Asia. These transactions, the theme of sharp contention at the time, were cast into the shade by events in which we were concerned in Egypt, our newly acquired interests in the Suez Canal making that country far more important to us than of yore. Its condition was very wretched, its government at once feeble and oppressive, and, despite the joint influence which France and England had acquired in Egyptian councils, an armed rebellion broke out, under the leadership of Arabi Pasha. France declining to act in this emergency, the troops and fleet of England put down this revolt single-handed; and in their successes the Queen's third son, Arthur, Duke of Connaught, took his part, under the orders of Sir Garnet (afterwards Lord) Wolseley. There were again rejoicings in Balmoral, where the Queen, with her soldierly son's young wife beside her, was preparing to receive another bride—Princess Helen of Waldeck, just wedded to our youngest Prince, Leopold, Duke of Albany.

But this gleam of brightness was destined to be followed by darker disaster far than that which seemed averted for the moment. A mightier rebellion was arising in the Soudan, a vast tract of country annexed by the ambition of Ismail, the former Khedive of Egypt, to be ill governed by his officials and ravaged by the slave-trade. These evils were checked for a few years by the strong hand of Charles George Gordon, already famous through his achievements in China, and invested with unlimited power by Ismail; but, that potentate being overthrown, the great Englishman left his thankless post, no longer tenable by him. Then it seemed that chaos had come again; and a bold and keen, though probably hypocritical, dervish, self-styled the *Mahdi*, or Mohammedan Messiah, was able to kindle new flames of revolt, which burned with the quenchless fury of Oriental fanaticism. His Arab and negro soldiers made short work of the poor Egyptian fellaheen sent to fight them, though these were under the command of Englishmen. The army led by Hicks Pasha utterly vanished in the deserts, as that of Cambyses did of old. The army under Baker Pasha did not, indeed, disappear in the same mysterious manner, but it too was routed with great slaughter.

The English Government, willing to avoid the vast task of crushing the revolt, had counselled the abandonment of the Soudan, and the Khedive's Ministers reluctantly acquiesced. But there were Egyptian garrisons scattered throughout the Soudan which must not be abandoned with the country. Above all, there was Khartoum, an important town at the junction of the Blue and the White Nile, with a large European settlement and an Egyptian garrison, all in pressing danger, loyal as yet, but full of just apprehension. These troops, these officials, these women and children, who only occupied their perilous position through the action of the Khedive's Government, had a right to protection—a right acknowledged by Her Majesty's Ministers; but they wished to avoid hostilities. General Graham, left in command on the Red Sea littoral, was allowed to take action against the Mahdi's lieutenant who was threatening Suakim, and who was driven back with heavy loss; but he might not follow up the victory.

The English Government hoped to withdraw the garrisons in safety, without force of arms. They had been for some time urging on the Khedive that the marvellous influence which Gordon was known to have acquired in his old province should now be utilised, and that to *him* should be entrusted the herculean task of tranquillising the Soudan, by reinstating its ancient dynasties of tribal chiefs and withdrawing all Egyptian and European troops and officials. Their plan was at last accepted; then Gordon, hitherto unacquainted, like the public at large, with the Government designs, was informed of them and invited to carry them out. He consented; and, with the chivalric promptitude which essentially belonged to his character, he departed the same night on his perilous errand. Passing through Cairo, he received plenary powers from the Khedive, and went on almost alone to Khartoum, where he was received with an overflowing enthusiasm. But, with all his eager haste, he was too late to bring about the desired results by peaceful means. "He should have come a year ago," muttered his native well-wishers. Week after week and month after month, his position in Khartoum became more perilous; the Mahdi's power waxed greater, and his hordes drew round the city, which long defied them, while garrison after garrison fell into their hands elsewhere. It was in vain that General Gordon urged the despatch of British troops, a few hundred of whom would at one time have sufficed to turn the tide, and insure success in his enterprise. They were still withheld; and he would not secure his own safety by deserting the people whom his presence had induced to stand out against the impostor and his hosts. The city endured a long, cruel siege, and fell at last, reduced by hunger and treachery, just as a tardily despatched British force was making its way to relieve it—a force commanded by Lord Wolseley, who half a year before had been protesting against the "indelible disgrace" of leaving Gordon to his fate. He was not able even to bury his friend and comrade, slain by the fanatic enemy when they broke into the city in the early morning of January 26th, 1885.

"I have done my best for the honour of our country," were the parting words of the dead hero. His country felt itself profoundly dishonoured by the manner in which it had lost this its famous son—a man distinguished at once by commanding ability, unsullied honour, heroic valour; a man full of tenderest beneficence towards his fellows, and of utter devotion to his God; "the grandest figure," said an American admirer, "that has crossed the disc of this planet for centuries." Him England had fatally delayed to help, withheld by the dread of costly and cruel warfare; and then just failed to save him by a war enormously costly and cruelly fatal indeed. A general lamentation, blent with cries of anger, rose up from the land. Her Majesty shared the common sorrow, as her messages of sympathy to the surviving relations of Gordon testified. Various charitable institutions, modelled on the lines which he had followed in his work among the poor, rose to keep his memory green; and thus the objects of his Christlike care during his life are now profiting by the world-famous manner of his death. But there is still a deep feeling that even time itself can hardly efface the stain that has been left on our national fame. An English expedition, well commanded, full of ardour and daring, sent to accomplish a specific object, and failing in that object; its commander, entirely guiltless of blame, having to abandon the scene of his triumphs to a savage, fanatic foe as was now the case—this was evil enough; but that our beloved countryman, a true knight without fear and without reproach, should have been betrayed to desertion and death through his own magnanimity and our sluggishness, added a rankling, poisonous sense of shame to our humiliation. That the same year saw further electoral privileges extended to the humble classes in England, beyond what

Anne E. Keeling

even the last Reform Bill had conferred, which might prove of advantage afterwards, but was an imperfect consolation at the time. Another grief fell upon the Queen in this year in the early death of Leopold, Duke of Albany, a Prince whose intellectual gifts were nearly allied to those of his father, but on whom lifelong delicacy of health had enforced a life of comparative quietude. His widowed bride and infant children have ever since been cared for tenderly by his royal mother.

CHAPTER VIII

OUR COLONIES

If now we turn our eyes a while from the foreign and domestic concerns of Great Britain proper, and look to the Greater Britain beyond the seas, we shall find that its progress has nowise lagged behind that of the mother Isle. To Lord Durham, the remarkable man sent out in 1838 to deal with the rebellion in Lower Canada, we owe the inauguration of a totally new scheme of colonial policy, which has been crowned with success wherever it has been introduced. It has succeeded in the vast Canadian Dominion, now stretching from ocean to ocean, and embracing all British North America, with the single exception of the Isle of Newfoundland. In 1867 this Federation was first formed, uniting then only the two Canadas with New Brunswick and Nova Scotia, under a constitution framed on Lord Durham's plan, and providing for the management of common affairs by a central Parliament, while each province should have its own local legislature, and the executive be vested in the Crown, ruling through its Governor General. It had been made competent for the other provinces of British North America to join this Federation, if they should so will; and one after another has joined it, with the one exception mentioned above, which may or may not be permanent. The population of the Dominion has trebled, and its revenues

Anne E. Keeling

have increased twenty-fold, since its constitution was thus settled.

The same system, it may be hoped, will equally succeed in that wonderful Australasia where our colonists now have the shaping of their destinies in their own hands, amid the yet unexplored amplitude of a land where "in the softest and sweetest air, and in an unexhausted soil, the fable of Midas is reversed; food does not turn to gold, but the gold with which the land is teeming converts itself into farms and vineyards, into flocks and herds, into crops of wild luxuriance, into cities whose recent origin is concealed and compensated by trees and flowers."

In such terms does a recent eye-witness describe the splendid prosperity attained within the last two or three decades by that Australia which our fathers thought of chiefly as a kind of far-off rubbish-heap where they could fling out the human garbage of England, to rot or redeem itself as it might, well out of the way of society's fastidious nostril, and which to our childhood was chiefly associated with the wild gold-fever and the wreck and ruin which that fever too often wrought. The transportation system, so far as Australia was concerned, came virtually to an end with the discovery of gold in the region to which we had been shipping off our criminals. The colonists had long been complaining of this system, which at first sight had much to recommend it, as offering a fair chance of reformation to the convict, and providing cheap labour for the land that received him. But it was found, as a high official said, that convict labour was far less valuable than the uncompelled work of honest freemen; and the contagious vices which the criminal classes brought with them made them little welcome. When to these drawbacks were added the difficulties and dangers with which the presence of the convict element in the population encumbered the new gold-mining industry, the question reached the burning stage. The system was modified in 1853, and totally abolished in 1857. Transports whose sentence were unexpired lingered out their time in Tasmania, whence the aborigines have vanished under circumstances of cruelty assuredly not mitigated by the presence of convicts in the island; but Australia was henceforth free from the blight.

The political life of these colonies may be said to have begun in the same year—1853—when the importation of criminals received its first check. New South Wales, the eldest of the Australian provinces, received a genuine constitution of its own; Victoria followed in 1856—Victoria, which is not without its dreams of being one day "the chief State in a federated Australia," an Australia that may then rank as "a second United States of the Southern Hemisphere." Western Australia, South Australia, Queensland, Tasmania, and New Zealand, one after another, attained the same liberties; all have now representative governments, modelled on those of the mother country, but inevitably without the aristocratic element. Such an aristocracy as that of England is the natural growth of many centuries and of circumstances hardly likely to be duplicated—a fact which the Prince Consort once had occasion to lay very clearly before Louis Napoleon, anxious to surround himself with a similar nobility, if only he could manage it. But though the aristocratic element be lacking, the patriotic passion and the sentiment of loyalty are abundantly present; nor has the mother country any intellectual pre-eminence over her colonies, drawn immeasurably nearer to her in thought and feeling as communication has become rapid and easy.

There is something almost magical at first sight in the transformation which the Australian colonies have under-gone in a very limited space of time; yet it is but the natural result of the untrammelled energy of a race sovereignly fitted to "subdue the earth." It is curious to read how in 1810 the convict settlement at Botany Bay—name of terror to ignorant home criminals, shuddering at the long, dreadful voyage and the imagined horrors of a savage country—was almost entirely nourished on imported food, now that the vast flocks and herds of Australia and New Zealand contribute no inconsiderable proportion of the food supply of Britain.

The record of New Zealand is somewhat less brilliant than that of its gigantic neighbour. This is due to somewhat less favourable circumstances, to a nobler and less manageable race of aborigines; the land perhaps more beautiful, is by the very character of its beauty less subduable. Its political life is at least as old as that of the old Australian colony, its constitution being granted about the same time; but this colony has needed, what Australia has not, the armed interference of the Home Government in its quarrels with the natives—a race once bold and warlike, able to hold their own awhile even against the English soldiers, gifted with eloquence, with a certain poetic imagination, and no inconsiderable intelligence. It seemed, too, at one moment as if these Maoris would become generally Christianised; but the kind of Christianity which they saw exemplified in certain colonists, hungry for land and little scrupulous as to the means by which they could gratify that hunger, largely undid the good effected through the agency of missionaries, the countrymen of these oppressors, whose evil deeds they were helpless to hinder. A superstition that was nothing Christian laid hold of many who had once been altogether persuaded to embrace the teachings of Jesus, and the relapsed Maoris doubtless were guilty of savage excesses; yet the original blame lay not chiefly with them; nor is it possible to regard without deep pity the spectacle presented at the present day of "the noblest of all the savage races with whom we have ever been brought in contact, overcome by a worse enemy than sword and bullet, and corrupted into sloth and ruin,

...ruined physically, demoralised in character, by drink." Nobler than other aborigines, who have faded out before the invasion of the white man, as they may be, their savage nobility has not saved them from the common fate; they too have "learned our vices faster than our virtues," aided by the speculative traders in alcoholic poison, who have followed on the track of the colonist, and who, devil's missionaries as they are, have counteracted too quickly the work of the Christian evangelists who preceded them.

The extraordinary natural fertility of the country, whose volcanic nature was very recently terribly demonstrated, is yet very far from being utilised to the utmost, the population of the islands, not inferior in extent to Great Britain, being yet a long way below that of London. Probably this "desert treasure-house of agricultural wealth" may, under wise self-government, yet rise to a position of magnificent importance.

Of all our colonies that in Southern Africa has the least reason to be proud of its recent history, which has not been rendered any fairer by the discovery of the great Diamond Fields, and the rush of all sorts and conditions of men to profit thereby. Into the entangled history of our doings in relation to Cape Colony—originally a Dutch settlement—and all our varied and often disastrous dealings with the Dutch-descended Boers and the native tribes in its neighbourhood, we cannot well enter. Our missionary action has the glory of great achievement in Southern Africa; of our political action it is best to say little.

A more encouraging scene is presented if we turn to the Fijian Isles, whose natives, once a proverb of cannibal ferocity, have been humanised and Christianised by untiring missionary effort, and by their own free-will have passed under British domination and are ruled by a British governor. The extraordinary change worked in the people of these isles, characterised now, as even in their heathen days, by a certain bold manliness, that hitherto has escaped the usual deterioration, is so great and unmistakable that critics predisposed to unfriendliness do not try to deny it.

In consequence of the immensely increased facilities of communication that we now enjoy, our own great food-producing dependencies and the vast corn-growing districts of other lands can pour their stores into our market—a process much aided by the successive removal of so many restrictions on commerce, and by the practical science which has overcome so many difficulties connected with the transport of slain meat and other perishable commodities. England seems not unlikely to become a wonderfully cheap country to live in, unless some new turn of events interferes with the processes which during the last two decades have so increased the purchasing power of money that, as is confidently stated, fifteen shillings will now buy what it needed twenty shillings to purchase twenty years ago. To this result, as a matter of course, the enormous development of our manufacturing and other industries has also contributed.

There is another side to the medal, and not so fair a one. The necessaries of life are cheaper; wages are actually higher, when the greater value of money is taken into account; more care is taken as to the housing of the poor; the workers of the nation have more leisure, and spend not a little of it in travelling, being now by far the most numerous patrons of the railway; the altered style of the conveyances provided for them is a sufficient testimony to their higher importance. All this is to the good; so, too, is the diminution in losses by bankruptcy and in general pauperism, the increasing thrift shown by the records of savings banks, the lengthening of life, the falling off in crime, which is actually—not proportionally—rarer than ten years ago, to go no further back.

Against this we have to set the facts that the terrible malady of insanity is distinctly on the increase—whether due to mere physical causes, to the high pressure at which modern society lives, or to the prevalent scepticisms which leave many wretched men so little tranquillising hope or faith, who shall say?—that all trades and professions are more or less overcrowded; and that there is a terrible amount, not of pauperism, but of hard-struggling poverty, massed up in the crowded, wretched, but high-priced tenements of great towns, and maintaining a forlorn life by such incessant, cruel labour as is not exacted from convicted criminals in any English prison. London, where this kind of misery is inevitably at its height, receives every week an accession of a thousand persons, who doubtless, in a great majority of cases, simply help to glut the already crowded labour market and still further lower the wages of the workers; and the other great towns in like manner grow, while the rural population remains stagnant or lessens. Agricultural distress, which helps to keep the tide of emigration high, also accounts in part for this singular, undesirable displacement of population; while recent testimony points to the fact that the terribly unsanitary and inefficient housing of the rural poor does much to drive the best and most laborious members of that class away from the villages and fields which might otherwise be the homes of happy and peaceful industry. For this form of evil, in town and country, private greed—frequently shown by small proprietors, who have never learnt that property has duties as well as rights—is very largely responsible; for how many other of the evils we have to deplore is not the greed of gain responsible?

The sins of the age are still much the same sins that the Laureate roughly arraigned when the Crimean war broke our long peace; denouncing the race for riches which turned men into "pickpockets, each hand lusting for all that is not its own;" denouncing the cruel selfishness of rich and poor as

Anne E. Keeling

the vilest kind of civil war, being "underhand, not openly bearing the sword." We had made the blessings of peace a curse, he told us, in those days, "when only the ledger lived, and when only not all men lied; when the poor were hovelled and hustled together, each sex, like swine; when chalk and alum and plaster were sold to the poor for bread, and the spirit of murder worked in the very means of life." Yet those very days saw the uprising of a whole generation of noble servants of humanity, resolute to tight and overcome the rampant evils that surrounded them. And though we would avoid the error of praising our own epoch as though it alone were humane, as though we only, "the latest seed of Time, have loved the people well," and shown our love by deeds; though we would not deny that to-day has its crying abuses as well as yesterday; yet it is hardly possible to survey the broad course of our history during the past sixty years, and not to perceive, amid all the cross-currents—false ambitions, false pretences, mammon-worship, pitiless selfishness, sins of individuals, sins of society, sins of the nation—an ever-widening and mastering stream of beneficent energy, which has already wonderfully changed for the better many of the conditions of existence, and which, since its flow shows no signs of abating, we may hope to see spreading more widely, and bearing down in its great flood the wrecks of many another oppression and iniquity.

CHAPTER IX

INTELLECTUAL AND SPIRITUAL PROGRESS

"Man doth not live by bread alone." The enormous material progress of this country during the last sixty years—imperfectly indicated by the fact that during the last forty years the taxable income of the United Kingdom has been considerably more than doubled—would be but a barren theme of rejoicing, if there were signs among us of intellectual or spiritual degeneracy. The great periods of English history have been always fruitful in great thinkers and great writers, in religious and mental activity. Endeavouring to judge our own period by this standard, and making a swift survey of its achievements in literature, we do not find it apparently inferior to the splendours of "great Elizabeth" or of the Augustan age of Anne. Our fifth Queen-regnant, whose reign, longer than that of any of her four predecessors, is also happier than that of the greatest among them, can reckon among her subjects an even larger number of men eminent in all departments of knowledge, though perhaps we cannot boast one name quite equal to Newton in science, and though assuredly neither this nor any modern nation has yet a second imaginative writer whose throne may be set beside that of Shakespeare.

We excel in quantity, indeed; for while, owing to the spread

Anne E. Keeling

of education, the number of readers has been greatly increased, the number of writers has risen proportionately; the activity of the press has increased tenfold. Journalism has become a far more formidable power in the land than in the earlier years when, as our domestic annals plainly indicate, the *Times* ruled as the Napoleon of newspapers. This result is largely due to the removal of the duties formerly imposed both on the journals themselves and on their essential paper material; and it would indeed "dizzy the arithmetic of memory" should we try to enumerate the varied periodicals that are far younger than Her Majesty's happy reign. Of these a great number are excellent in both intention and execution, and must be numbered among the educating, civilising, Christianising agencies of the day. They are something more and higher than the "savoury literary *entremets*" designed to please the fastidious taste of a cultured and leisured class, which was the just description of our periodical literature at large not so very long ago. The number of our imaginative writers—poets and romancers, but especially the latter—has been out of all proportion great. We give the place of honour, as is their due, to the singers rather than to the story-tellers, the more readily since the popular taste, it cannot be denied, chooses its favourites in inverse order as a rule.

When Her Majesty ascended the throne, one brilliant poetical constellation was setting slowly, star by star. Keats and Shelley and Byron, none of them much older than the century, had perished in their early prime between 1820 and 1824; Scott had sunk under the storms of fortune in 1832; the fitful glimmer of Coleridge's genius vanished in 1834, and a year later "the gentle Elia" too was gone. Southey, who still held the laureate-ship in 1837, had faded out of life in 1843, and was succeeded in his once-despised office by William Wordsworth, who, with Rogers and Leigh Hunt and Moore, lived far into the new reign, uniting the Georgian and the Victorian school of writers. Thomas Hood, the poet of the poor and oppressed, whose too short life ended in 1845, gives in his serious verse such thrilling expression to the impassioned, indignant philanthropy, which has actuated many workers and writers of our own period, that it is not easy to reckon him with the older group. His song rings like that of Charles Kingsley, poet, novelist, preacher, and "Christian socialist," who did not publish his "Saint's Tragedy" till three years after Hood was dead.

There has, indeed, been no break in the continuity of our great literary history; while one splendid group was setting, another as illustrious was rising. Tennyson, who on Wordsworth's death in 1850 received at Queen Victoria's hand the "laurel greener from the brows of him that uttered nothing base," had published his earliest two volumes of poems some years before Her Majesty's accession; and of that rare poetic pair, the Brownings, each had already given evidence of the great powers they possessed, Robert Browning's tragedy of "Strafford" being produced on the stage in 1837, while his future wife's translation of the "Prometheus Bound" saw the light four years earlier. The Victorian period can boast no greater poetic names than these, each of which is held in highest reverence by its own special admirers. The patriotic fervour with which Lord Tennyson has done almost all his laureate work, the lucid splendour of his style, the perfect music of his rhythm, and the stinging sharpness with which he has sometimes chastised contemporary sins, have all combined to win for him a far wider popularity than even that accorded to the fine lyrical passion of Mrs. Browning, or to the deep-thoughted and splendid, but often perplexing and ruggedly phrased, dramatic and lyric utterances of her husband. All three have honoured themselves and their country by a majestic purity of moral and religious teaching —an excellence shared by many of their contemporaries, whose powers would have won them a first place in an age and country less fruitful of genius; but not so conspicuous in

Anne E. Keeling

some younger poets, later heirs of fame, whose lot it may be to carry on the traditions of Victorian greatness into another reign.

There are not a few writers of our day whose excellent prose work has won more of popular favour than their verse, which notwithstanding is of high quality. Such was the "unsub-duable old Roman," Walter Savage Landor, a contemporary of Byron and Wordsworth, who long outlived them, dying in 1864. Such—to bring two extremes together—are the critic and poet Matthew Arnold, the poet and theologian John Henry Newman. Intimately associated in our thought with the latter, who has enriched our devotional poetry with one touching hymn, is Keble, the singer *par excellence* of the "Catholic revival," and the most widely successful religious poet of the age, though only very few of his hymns have reached the heart of the people like the far more direct and fervent work of the Wesleys and their compeers. He is even excelled in simplicity and passion, though not in grace and tenderness, by two or three other workers in the same field, who belong to our day, and whose verse is known more widely than their names.

We have several women-poets who are only less beloved and less well known than Mrs. Browning; but so far the greatest literary distinction gained by the women of our age and country, notwithstanding the far wider and higher educa-tional advantages enjoyed by them to-day, has been won, as of yore, in the field of prose fiction. More than a hundred years ago a veteran novelist, whose humour and observation, something redeeming his coarseness, have ranked him among classic English authors, referred mischievously to the engrossing of "that branch of business" by female writers, whose "ease, and spirit, and delicacy, and knowledge of the human heart," have not, however, availed to redeem their names from oblivion. For some of their nineteenth-century successors at least we may expect a more enduring memory.

Numerous as are our poets, they are far outnumbered by the novelists, whose works are poured forth every season with bewildering profusion; but as story-tellers have always commanded a larger audience than grave philosophers or historians, and as our singers deal as much in philosophy as in narrative, perhaps in seeking for the cause of this overrunning flood of fiction we need go no further than the immensely increased number of readers—a view in which the records of some English public libraries will bear us out. We may therefore be thankful that, on the whole, such literature has been of a vastly purer and healthier character than of yore, reflecting that higher and better tone of public feeling which we may attribute, in part at least, to the influence of the "pure court and serene life" of the Sovereign.

This nobler tone is not least perceptible in the eldest of the great masters of fiction whom we can claim for our period— Dickens, who in 1837 first won by his "Pickwick Papers" that astonishing popularity which continued widening until his death; Thackeray, who in that year was working more obscurely, having not yet found a congenial field in the humorous chronicle that reflects for us so much of the Victorian age, for *Punch* was not started till 1841, and Thackeray's first great masterpiece of pathos and satire, "Vanity Fair," did not begin to appear till five years later. Each of these writers in his own way held "the mirror up" to English human nature, and showed "the very age and body of the time his form and pressure," with manly boldness indeed, but with due artistic reticence also; each knew how to be vivid without being vicious, to be realistic without being revolting; and despite the sometimes offensive caricature in which the one indulged, despite the seeming cynicism of the other their influence must be pronounced healthy. Thackeray

Anne E. Keeling

did not, like Dickens, use his pen against particular glaring abuses of the time, nor insist on the special virtues that bloom amid the poor and lowly; but he attacked valiantly the crying sins of society in all time—the mammon-worship and the mercilessness, the false pretences and the fraud—and never failed to uphold for admiration and imitation "whatsoever things are true, whatsoever things are honourable, whatsoever things are just, whatsoever thing are pure, whatsoever things are lovely." And though both writers were sometimes hard on the professors of religion, neither failed in reverence of tone when religion itself was concerned.

The sudden death of both these men, in the very prime of life and in the fulness of power, was keenly felt at the time: each had a world-wide fame, and each awakened a blank, distressful sense of personal loss in his many admirers as he was suddenly called away from incomplete work and faithful friendship. Contemporary literature has not benefited by the removal of these two men and the gradual diminishing of the influence they so strongly exerted while yet they "stood up and spoke." The work of Charlotte Bronte—produced under a fervent admiration for "the satirist of Vanity Fair," whom she deemed "the first social regenerator of his day"—is, with all its occasional morbidness of sensitive feeling, far more bracing in moral tone, more inspiring in its scorn of baseness and glorifying of goodness, than is the work of recent Positivist emulators of the achievements of George Eliot. Some romances of this school are vivid and highly finished pictures of human misery, unredeemed by hope, and hardly brightened by occasional gleams of humour, of the sardonic sort which may stir a mirthless smile, but never a laugh. Herein they are far inferior to their model, whose melancholy philosophy is half hidden from her readers by the delightful freshness and truth of her "Dutch painter's" portraying of every-day humanity, by her delicately skilful reproduction of its homely wit and harmless absurdity.

Happily neither these writers, nor the purveyors of mere sensation who cannot get on without crime and mystery, exhaust the list of our romancers, many of whom are altogether healthful, cheerful, and helpful; and it is no unreasonable hope that these may increase and their gloomier rivals decrease, or at least grow gayer and wiser.

There are many other great writers, working in other fields, whom we may claim as belonging altogether or almost to the Victorian age. Within that period lies almost entirely the brilliantly successful career of Macaulay, essayist, poet, orator, and historian. For the last-named *role* Macaulay seemed sovereignly fitted by his extraordinary faculty for assimilating and retaining historical knowledge, and by the vividness of imagination and mastery of words which enabled him to present his facts in such attractive guise as made them fascinating far beyond romance. His "History of England from the Accession of James II," whereof the first volumes appeared in 1849, remains a colossal fragment; the fulness of detail with which he adorned it, the grand scale on which he worked, rendered its completion a task almost impossible for the longest lifetime; and Macaulay died in his sixtieth year. Despite the defects of partisanship and exaggeration freely and not quite unjustly charged upon his great work, it remains a yet unequalled record of the period dealt with, just as his stirring ballads, so seemingly easy of imitation in their ringing, rolling numbers, hold their own against very able rivals and are yet unequalled in our time.

Macaulay was not the first, and he is not the last, of our picturesque historians. It was in 1837 that Carlyle, who four years before had startled the English-reading public by his strangely worded, bewildering "Sartor Resartus," brought out his astonishing "History of the French Revolution"—a prose poem, an epic without a hero, revealing as by "flashes of lightning" the ghastly tragedy and comedy of that

Anne E. Keeling

tremendous upheaval; and in 1845 he followed up the vein thus opened by his lifelike study of "Oliver Cromwell," which was better received by his English readers than the later "History of Friedrich II," marvel of careful research and graphic reproduction though it be. To Carlyle therefore and to Macaulay belongs the honour of having given a new and powerful impulse to the study they adorned; dissimilar in other respects, they are alike in their preference for and insistent use of original sources of information, in their able employment of minute detail, and in the graphic touch and artistic power which made history very differently attractive in their hands from what it had ever been previously. Mr. Froude and Mr. Green may be ranked as their followers in this latter respect; hardly so Mr. Freeman or the philosophic Buckle, Grote, and Lecky, who by their style and method belong more to the school of Hallam, however widely they may differ from him or from each other in opinion. But in thoroughness of research and in resolute following of the very truth through all mazes and veils that may obscure it, one group of historians does not yield to the other.

And the same zealous passion for accuracy that has distinguished these and less famous historians and biographers has shown itself in other fields of intellectual endeavour. Our Queen in her desire "to get at the root and reality of things" is entirely in harmony with the spirit of her age. In scientific men we look for the ardent pursuit of difficult truth; and it would be thankless to forget how numerous beyond precedent have been in the Victorian period faithful workers in the field of science. Though some of our *savants* in later years have injured their renown by straying outside the sphere in which they are honoured and useful and speaking unadvisedly on matters theological, this ought not to deter us from acknowledging the value of true service rendered. The Queen's reign can claim as its own such men as John Herschel, worthy son of an illustrious father, Airy, Adams, and Maxwell, Whewell and Brewster and Faraday, Owen and Buckland and Lyell, Murchison and Miller, Darwin and Tyndall and Huxley, with Wheatstone, one of the three independent inventors of telegraphy, and the Stephensons, father and son, to whose ability and energy we are indebted for the origination and perfection of our method of steam locomotion; it can boast such masters in philosophy as Hamilton and Whately and John Stuart Mill, each a leader of many. It has also the rare distinction of possessing one lady writer on science who has attained to real eminence— eminence not likely soon to be surpassed by her younger sister-rivals—the late Mrs. Mary Somerville, who united an entirely feminine and gentle character to masculine powers of mind.

Only to catalogue the recent discoveries and inventions we owe to men of science, from merciful anaesthetics to the latest applications of electric power, would occupy more space than we ought here to give. All honour to these servants of humanity! We rejoice to find among them many who could unite the simplest childlike faith with a wide and grand mental outlook; we exult not less to find in many Biblical students and commentators the same patience, thoroughness, and resolute pursuit of the very truth as that exemplified by the devotees of physical science. God's Word is explored in our day—the same clay which has seen the great work of the Revised Version of the Scriptures begun and completed—with no less ardour than God's world. And what vast additions have been made to our knowledge of this earth! We have seen Nineveh unburied, the North-West Passage explored, and the mysterious Nile stream at last tracked to its source. To compare a fifty-years-old map of Africa with one of the present day will a little enable us to estimate the advances made in our acquaintance with the Dark Continent alone; similar maps including the Polar regions of North America will testify also to a large increase

Anne E. Keeling

of hard-won knowledge.

Exploration—Arctic, African, Oriental and Occidental—has had its heroic devotees, sometimes its martyrs. Witness Franklin, Burke and Wills, and Livingstone. The long uncertainty overhanging the fate of the gallant Franklin, after he and the expedition he commanded had vanished into the darkness of Arctic winter in 1845, and the unfaltering faithfulness with which his widow clung to the search for her lost husband, form one of the most pathetic chapters of English story. The veil was lifted at last and the secret of the North-West Passage, to which so many lives had been sacrificed, was brought to light in the course of the many efforts made to find the dead discoverer. As Franklin had disappeared in the North, so Livingstone was long lost to sight in the wilds of Africa, and hardly less feverish interest centred round the point, so long disputed, of his being in life or in death—interest freshly awakened when the remains of the heroic explorer, who had been found only to be lost again, were brought home to be laid among the mighty dead of England. The fervent Christian philanthropy of Livingstone endeared him yet more to the national heart; and we may here note that very often, as in his case, the missionary has served not only Christianity, as was his first and last aim, but also geographical and ethnological science and colonial and commercial development. We have briefly referred already to some of the struggles, the sufferings, and the triumphs of missionary enterprise in our day: to chronicle all its effort and achievement would be difficult, for these have been world-wide, and often wonderfully successful. Nor has much less success crowned other agencies for meeting the ever-increasing need for religious knowledge, which multiply and grow in number and in power. Witness, among many that might be named, the continuous development of the Sunday School system and the immensely extended operations of the unsectarian Bible Society.

Great advances have been made during this reign in English art and art-criticism, and more particularly in the extension of real artistic education to classes of the community who could hardly attain it before, though it was perhaps more essential to them than to the wealthy and leisurely who had previously monopolised it. The multiplication of Schools of Design over the country, intended to promote the tasteful efficiency of those engaged in textile manufactures and in our decorative and constructive art generally, is one remarkable feature of the time, and the sedulous cultivation of music by members of all classes of society is another, hardly less hopeful. In all these efforts for the benefit and elevation of the community the Prince Consort took deep and active interest, and the royal family themselves, from Her Majesty downwards, highly cultured and accomplished, have not failed to act in the same spirit. But the history of English nineteenth-century art would be incomplete indeed without reference to two powerful influences—the rise and progress of the new art of photography, which has singularly affected other branches of graphic work; and the career, hitherto unexampled in our land, of the greatest art-critic of this, perhaps of any, age—John Ruskin, the most eminent also of the many writers and thinkers who have been swayed by the magic spell of Carlyle, whose fierce and fervid genius, for good or for evil, told so strongly on his contemporaries. Ruskin is yet more deeply imbued with his master's philosophy than those other gifted and widely influential teachers, Maurice and Kingsley; and yet perhaps he is more strongly and sturdily independent in his individuality than either, while the unmatched English of his prose style differs not less widely from the rugged strength of Carlyle than from the mystical involution of Maurice and the vehement and, as it were, breathless, yet vivid and poetic, utterance of Kingsley. When every defect has been admitted that is chargeable against one or all of this group of sincere and stalwart workers, it must be allowed that their power on their countrymen has been largely wielded for good. Particularly is this the case with Ruskin, whose influence has reached and ennobled many a life that, from pressure of sordid circumstances, was in great need of such help as his spirituality of tone, and deeply felt reverential belief in the Giver of all good and Maker of all beauty, could afford.

We have preferred not to dwell on one department of literature which, like every other, has received great additions during our period—that of religious controversy. A large portion of such literature is in its very nature ephemeral; and some of the disputes which have engaged the energies even of our greatest masters in dialectics have not been in themselves of supreme importance; but many points of doctrine and discipline have been violently canvassed among professing Christians, and attacks of long-sustained vigour and virulence have been made on almost every leading article of the Christian creed by the avowed enemies or the only half-hostile critics of the Church, which the champions of Scripture truth have not been backward to repel. Amid all this confusion and strife of assault and resistance one thing stands out clearly: Christianity and its progress are more interesting to the national mind than ever before. It has been well, too, that through all those fifty years a large-minded and fervent but most unobtrusive and practical piety has been enthroned in the highest places of the land—a piety which will escape the condemnation of the King when He shall come in His glory, and say to many false followers, "I was an hungred, and ye gave Me no meat; I was thirsty, and ye gave Me no drink; I was a stranger, and ye took Me not in; naked, and ye clothed Me not; sick, and in prison, and ye visited Me not."

These dread words are not for those who have cared as our Sovereign Lady and her beloved ones have cared for the sick and the suffering and the sad; who have bound up the heart-wounds of the widow and the orphan and ministered to their earthly needs; who, like our lost Princess Alice and her royal elder sister, have tended the victims of war, shrinking from no ghastliness or repulsiveness, no horrors of the hospital where victor and vanquished lay moaning in common misery; or, like their queenly mother, have shed the sunshine of royal smiles and soothing words and helpful alms upon the obscurer but hardly less pitiable patients who crowd our English infirmaries. In her northern and southern "homes" of Osborne and Balmoral the Queen, too, has been able to share a true, unsophisticated friendship with her humble neighbours, to rejoice in their joys and lighten their griefs with gentle, most efficient sympathy. It was of a Highland cottage that Dr. Guthrie wrote that "within its walls the Queen had stood, with her kind hands smoothing the thorns of a dying man's pillow. There, left alone with him at her own request, she had sat by the bed of death—a Queen ministering to the comfort of a saint." It was in a cottage at Osborne that the same gentle and august almsgiver was found reading comfortable Scripture words to a sick and aged peasant, quietly retiring upon the entrance of the clerical visitant, that *his* message of peace might be freely given, and thus allowing the sufferer to disclose to the pastor that the lady in the widow's weeds was Victoria of England. These are examples, which it would be easy to multiply, of that true oneness of feeling between the lofty and the lowly which is the special, the unique glory of Christ's kingdom. May our land never lack them; may they multiply themselves to all time.

The best evidence of the truth of the Gospel is admittedly its unequalled power of lifting up humanity to higher and yet higher levels. In many and mighty instances of that power our age is not barren. And in despite of the foes without and within that have wrought her woe—of the Pharisaism that is a mask for fraud, of the mammon-worship cloaked as respectability, of scepticism lightly mocking, of the bolder enmity of the blasphemer—we cannot contemplate the story of Christianity throughout our epoch, even in these islands and this empire, without seeing that the advance of the Faith is real and constant, the advance of the rising tide, and that her seeming defeats are but the deceptive reflux of the ever-mounting waves.

CHAPTER X

PROGRESS OF THE EMPIRE
FROM 1887 TO 1897

Resuming our pen after an interval of ten years, we have thought it well, not only to carry on our story of the Sovereign and her realm to the latest attainable point, but also to give some account of the advance made and the work accomplished by the Methodist Church, which, youngest of the greater Nonconformist denominations, has acted more powerfully than any other among them on the religious and social life, not only of the United Kingdom and the Empire, but of the world. This account, very brief, but giving details little known to outsiders, will form a valuable pendant to the sketch of the general history of Victoria's England that we are now about to continue.

Many thousands who rejoiced in the Queen's Jubilee of 1887 are glad to-day that the close of the decade should find the beloved Lady of these isles, true woman and true Queen, still living and reigning.

On September 23, 1896, Queen Victoria had reigned longer than any other English monarch, and the desire was general for some immediate celebration of the event; but, by the Queen's express wish, all recognition of the fact was deferred

Anne E. Keeling

until the sixtieth year should be fully completed, and the nation prepared to celebrate the "Diamond Jubilee" on June 22, 1897, with a fervour of loyalty that should far outshine that of the Jubilee year of 1887.

In the personal history of our Queen during those ten years we may note with reverent sympathy some events that must shadow the festival for her. The calm and kindly course of her home-life has again been broken in upon by bereavement. All seemed fair in the Jubilee year itself, and the Queen was appearing more in public than had been her wont—laying the foundations of the Imperial Institute; unveiling in Windsor Park a statue of the Prince Consort, Jubilee gift of the women of England; taking part in a magnificent naval review at Spithead. But a shadow was already visible to some; and early in 1888 sinister rumours were afloat as to the health of the Crown Prince of Germany, consort of the Queen's eldest daughter. Too soon those rumours proved true. Even when the prince rode in the splendid Jubilee procession, a commanding figure in his dazzling white uniform, the cruel malady had fastened on him that was to slay him in less than a year, proving fatal three months after the death of his aged father had called him to fill the imperial throne. The nation followed the course of this tragedy with a feverish interest never before excited by the lot of any foreign potentate, and deeply sympathised with, the distress of the Queen and of the bereaved empress.

But the year 1892 held in store a blow yet more cruelly felt. The English people were still rejoicing with the Queen over the betrothal of the Duke of Clarence, eldest son of the Prince of Wales, to his kinswoman Princess May of Teck, when the death of the bridegroom elect in January plunged court and people into mourning. That the Queen was greatly touched by the universal sympathy with her and hers was proved by the pathetic letter she wrote to the nation, and by the frank reliance on their affection which marked the second letter in which, eighteen months later, she asked them to share her joy in the wedding of the Duke of York, now heir-presumptive, to the bride-elect of his late brother. This union has been highly popular, and the Queen's evident delight in the birth of the little Prince Edward of York in June, 1894, touched the hearts of her subjects, who remembered the deep sorrow of 1892.

Once more they were called to grieve with her, when the husband of her youngest daughter Beatrice, Prince Henry of Battenberg, who for years had formed part of her immediate circle, died far from home and England, having fallen a victim to fever ere he could distinguish himself, as he had hoped, in our last expedition to Ashanti. The pathos of such a death was deeply felt when the prince's remains were brought home and laid to rest, in the presence of his widow and her royal mother, in the very church at Whippingham that he had entered an ardent bridegroom. Not all gloom, however, has been Her Majesty's domestic life in these recent years; she has taken joy in the marriages of many of her descendants; and the visits of her grandchildren—of whom one, Princess Alice of Hesse, daughter of the well-beloved Alice of England, became Czarina of Russia only the other day—are a source of keen interest to her.

But there is no selfish absorption in her own family affairs, no neglect of essential duty. The Prince of Wales and "the Princess" relieve the Queen of many irksome social functions; but she does not shun these when it is clear to her that her people wish her to undertake them. Witness her willingness to take part in the Jubilee Thanksgiving services and pageant, despite the feebleness of her advanced age.

We need not dwell long on the rather stormy Parliamentary history of the last decade, on the divisions and

Anne E. Keeling

disappointments of the Irish Home Rule party, once so powerful, or on the various attacks aimed at the Welsh and Scottish Church establishments and at the principle of "hereditary legislation" as embodied in the House of Lords. Some useful legislation has been accomplished amid all the strife. We may instance the Act in 1888 creating the new system of County Councils, the Parish Councils Act, the Factory and Workshops Amendment Act, and the Education Act of 1891—measures designed to protect the toiling millions from the evils of "sweating," and to assure their children of practically free education.

Substantial good has been done, whether the reins of power have been held by Mr. Gladstone or by Lord Salisbury— whose long tenure of office expiring in 1892, the veteran statesman whom he had displaced again took the helm—or by Lord Rosebery, in whose favour the great leader finally withdrew in 1894 into private life, weary of the burden of State. In 1897 we again see Lord Salisbury directing the destinies of the mighty empire—a task of exceptional difficulty, now that the gravest complications exist in Europe itself and in Africa. The horrors suffered by the Armenian subjects of the Turk have called for intervention by the great powers; but no sooner had Turkish reforms been promised in response to the joint note of Great Britain, France, and Russia, than new troubles began in Crete, its people rising in arms to shake off the Turkish yoke.

Meanwhile our occupation of Egypt is compelling us to use armed force against the wild, threatening dervishes in the Soudan, and well-grounded uneasiness is felt as to the position and action of our countrymen in Southeastern Africa in connexion with the Boer republic of the Transvaal. The British South Africa Chartered Company, formed in 1889, adventurous and ambitious, loomed large in men's eyes during 1896, when the historic and disastrous raid of Dr.

Jameson and his followers startled the civilised world. The whole story of that enterprise is yet to unfold; but it has added considerably to the embarrassments of the British government. Hopes were entertained in 1890 that the British East Africa Company, by the pressure it could put on the Sultan of Zanzibar, had secured the cessation of the slave trade on the East African shore; these hopes are not yet fulfilled, but it may be trusted that a step has been taken towards the mitigation of the evil—the "open sore of the world."

If we turn to India, we see it in 1896-7 still in the grip of a cruel famine, aggravated by an outbreak of the bubonic plague too well known to our fathers, which, appearing three years ago at Hong-Kong, has committed new ravages at Bombay. Government is making giant efforts to meet both evils, and is aided by large free-will offerings of money, sent not only from this country, but also from Canada. "Ten years ago such a manifestation would have been unlikely. The sense of kinship is stronger, the imperial sentiment has grown deeper, the feeling of responsibility has broadened." Kinship with a starving race is felt and shown by the Empress on her throne, and her subjects learn to follow her example.

But the sense of brotherhood seems somewhat deficient when we look at the continual labour wars that mark the period in our own land. From the Hyde Park riots of socialists and unemployed, in the end of 1887, to the railway strikes of 1897, the story is one of strikes among all sorts and conditions of workers, paralysing trade, and witnessing to strained relations between labour and capital; the great London strike of dock labourers, lasting five weeks, and keeping 2,500 men out of work, may yet be keenly remembered. There seems an imperative need for the wide diffusion of a true, practical Christianity among employers

Anne E. Keeling

and employed; some signs point to the growth of that healing spirit: and we may note with delight that while never was there so much wealth and never such deep poverty as during this period, never also were there so many religious and charitable organisations at work for the relief of poverty and the uplifting of the fallen; while not a few of the wealthy, and even one or two millionaires, have shown by generous giving their painful sense of the contrast between their own wealth and the destitution of others.

It has been a period of sharp religious disputes, and every religious and benevolent institution is keenly criticised; but great good is being done notwithstanding by devoted men and women. The centenary of the Baptist Missionary Society, observed in 1892, recalled to mind the vast work accomplished by missions since that pioneer society sent out the apostolic "shoemaker" Carey, to labour in India, and reminds us of the great change wrought in public opinion since he and his enterprise were so bitterly attacked. The heroic missionary spirit is still alive, as is proved by the readiness of new evangelists to step into the place of the missionaries to China, cruelly murdered at Ku-Cheng in 1895 by heathen fanatics.

The immense development of our colonies during the reign has already been noticed; some of them have made surprising advances during the last ten years. In southern and eastern Africa British enterprise has done much to develop the great natural wealth of the land; but the frequent troubles in Matabeleland and the complications with the Transvaal since the discovery of gold there may be regarded as counterbalancing the material advantages secured. Ceylon has a happier record, having more than regained her imperilled prosperity through the successful enterprise of her settlers in cultivating the fine tea which has almost displaced China tea in the British market, Ceylon exporting 100,000,000 lbs. in

1895 as against 2,000,000 lbs. ten years previously. Canada also now takes rank as a great maritime state, and the fortunes of Australia, though much shaken a few years ago by a great financial crisis, are again brilliant; in the world of social progress and democracy it is still the colonial marvel of our times.

The last census, taken in 1891, in Great Britain and Ireland showed a vast increase of population, sixty-two towns in England and Wales returning more than 50,000 inhabitants, and the total population of the United Kingdom being 38,104,975. Alarmists warned us that, with the ratio of increase shown, neither food nor place would soon be found for our people; and a great impetus being given to emigration, our colonies benefited. But despite such alarms, articles of luxury were in greater demand than ever, the tobacco duty reaching in 1892 the sum of L10,135,666, half a million, more than in the previous year; and the consumption of tea and spirits increased in due proportion. The same year saw great improvements in sanitation put into practice as the result of an alarm of cholera, that plague ravaging Hamburg.

Vast engineering works, of which the Manchester Ship Canal is the most familiar instance, have been carried on. This great waterway, thirty-five miles long, and placing an inland town in touch with the sea, was begun in 1887 and finished in 1894. Numerous exhibitions, at home and abroad, have stimulated industrial and aesthetic progress; and science has continued to advance with bewildering rapidity, developing chiefly in practical directions. The bacteriologist has unveiled much of the mystery of disease, showing that seed-germs produce it; the photographer comes in aid of surgery, for the discovery of the X or Roentgen rays, by the German professor whose name is associated with them, now enables the surgeon to discover foreign bodies lodged within the

Anne E. Keeling

human frame, and to decide with authority their position and the means of removing them. Burial reforms, in the interests of health and economy, have been introduced, and nursing, elevated into a science, has become an honourable profession for cultured women. In 1894 that eminent *savant* Lord Rayleigh brought before the British Association his discovery of a hitherto unknown constituent in the atmosphere. The use of steam as a motive power, almost contemporaneous with the Queen's reign, has bound our land in a network of railways: now it is electricity which is being utilised in the same sense, and to the telephone and the telegraph as means of verbal communication is added the motorcar as a means of rapid progression, 1896 seeing its use in streets sanctioned by Parliament. It may not yet supersede the bicycle, which in ten years has greatly increased in favour. Electric lighting, in the same period, has become very general; and further adaptations of this mysterious force to man's service are in the air.

This is an age of great explorers. Stanley has succeeded to Livingstone, Nansen to Franklin; but it has been only within comparatively recent years that women have emulated men in penetrating to remote regions. Within the decade we have seen Mrs. Bishop a veteran traveller, visiting south-west Persia; Mrs. French Sheldon has shown how far beyond the beaten track a woman's adventurous spirit may lead her; and Miss Mary Kingsley, a niece of the late Charles Kingsley, has intrepidly explored the interior of Africa, her scientific observations being welcomed by British *savants*. In 1896 women, who had long sought the privilege, were permitted to compete for the diploma of the Royal College of Surgeons, and in many other walks of usefulness the barriers excluding women have been removed, with benefit to all concerned. It is not other than natural that under the reign of a noble woman there should arise women noble-minded as herself, cherishing ideas of life and duty lofty as her own, and that their greatest elevation of purpose should tent to raise the moral standard among the men who work with them for the uplifting of their fellow subjects. Such signs of the times may be noticed now, more evident than even ten years ago.

The educational progress of the last decade has been very great, especially as regards the instruction of women; yet the period has not been noticeably fruitful of literature in the highest sense. In the world of fiction there is much that looks like degeneration; the lighter magazines and serials have multiplied past computation, and form all the reading of not a few persons. To counteract the unhealthy "modern novel" has arisen the Scottish school, the "literature of the kailyard," as it has been termed in scorn; yet a purer air breathes in the pages of J. M. Barrie, "Ian Maclaren," and Crockett. Their many imitators are in some danger of impairing the vogue of these masters, but still the tendency of the school is wholesome. Other artists in fiction assume the part of censors of society, and write of its doings with a bitterness that may or may not profit; the unveiling of cancerous sores is of doubtful advantage to health.

The death-roll from 1887 to 1897 is exceptionally heavy; in every department of science, art, literary and religious life, the loss has been great. Many musicians have been taken from us since the well-beloved Jenny Lind Goldschmidt; Canon Sir E. A. Gore Ouseley, Sir G. Macfarren, Principal of the Royal Academy of Music, Rubinstein, Carrodus, and others.

English letters have suffered by the removal of many whose services in one way or another have been great: the prose-painter Richard Jefferies; the pure and beneficent Mrs. Craik, better known as Miss Muloch; Matthew Arnold, poet, educationalist, critic, whose verse should outlive his criticisms; the noble astronomer Richard Proctor; Gustave Masson, the careful biographer of Milton; Laurence Oliphant, gifted and eccentric visionary; the naturalist J. G. Wood; the explorer and orientalist Burton; the historians Kinglake, Froude, and Freeman; the great ecclesiastics Bishop Lightfoot, Canon Liddon, Archbishop Magee of York, Dean Church, Dean Plumptre, and the Cardinals Newman and Manning; Tennyson and Browning, poets whose mantle has yet fallen on none; Huxley and Tyndall, eminent in science; the justly popular preacher and writer Charles H. Spurgeon; the orator and philanthropist John Bright, whose speeches delight many in book-form; and Robert Louis Stevenson, novelist, essayist, poet. To these we may add Eliza Cook and Martin Tapper, widely popular a generation ago, and surviving into our own day; Lord Lytton, known as "Owen Meredith," a literary artist, before he became viceroy of India and British ambassador at Paris; and Professor Henry Drummond, dead since 1897 began, and widely known by his "Natural Law in the Spiritual World." Even so our list is far from complete.

Of painters and sculptors we have lost since 1887 Frank Holl; Sir Edgar Boehm, buried in St. Paul's by express wish of the Queen; Edwin Long; John Pettie; Sir Noel Paton; Sir Frederick Leighton; and Sir J. E. Millais. The last two illustrious painters were successively Presidents of the Royal Academy, Millais, who followed Leighton in that office, surviving him but a short time. Sir Frederick had been raised to the peerage as Lord Leighton only a few days before he died, the patent arriving too late for him to receive it.

The English world is the poorer for these many losses, some of which took place under tragic circumstances; yet hope may well be cherished that amongst us are those, not yet fully recognised, who will nobly fill the places of the dead. Some hymn-writer may arise whose note will be as sweet as that of the much loved singer, Dr. Horatius Bonar, some painter as spiritual and powerful as Paton, some poet as grandly gifted as the late laureate and his compeer Browning. We do not at once recognise our greatest while they are with us; therefore we need not think despairingly of our age because the good and the great pass away, and we see not their place immediately filled. Nor, though there be great and crying evils in our midst, need we tremble lest these should prevail, while there is so much earnest and energetic endeavour to cope with and overcome them.

Anne E. Keeling

CHAPTER XI

PROGRESS OF WESLEYAN METHODISM
UNDER QUEEN VICTORIA, 1837-1897
[Footnote]

PART I

When the Queen ascended the throne Wesleyan Methodism in this country was recovering from the effects of the agitation occasioned by Dr. Warren, who had been expelled from its ministry; the erection of an organ in a Leeds chapel had caused another small secession. But the Conference of 1837, assembled in Leeds under the presidency of the Rev. Edmund Grindrod, with the Rev. Robert Newton as secretary, had no reason to be discouraged. Faithful to the loyal tradition of Methodism, it promptly attended to the duty of congratulating the young Sovereign who had ascended the throne on June 20, a few weeks before.

[Footnote: The writer desires to acknowledge special obligation to the Rev. J. Wesley Davies for invaluable aid rendered by him in collecting and arranging the material embodied in this chapter.]

We may read in its Minutes of the vote in favour of an

address, which should assure the Queen of the sincere attachment cherished by her Methodist subjects for her person and government, and of their fervent prayers to Almighty God "for her personal happiness and the prosperity of her reign." By a singular coincidence, it will probably be one of the first acts of a Leeds Conference in 1897 to forward another address, congratulating Her Majesty on the long and successful reign which has realised these aspirations of unaffected devotion. The address of 1837 had gracious acknowledgment, conveyed through Lord John Russell.

At this time Methodism had spread throughout the world. Its membership in Great Britain and Ireland numbered 318,716; in foreign mission stations 66,007; in Upper Canada 14,000; while the American Conferences had charge of 650,678 members; thus the total for the world, exclusive of ministers, was 1,049,401.

Of ministers there were 1,162 in the United Kingdom and 3,316 elsewhere. It will be obvious that British and Irish Methodism even then formed a body whose allegiance was highly valuable.

The 1837 Conference had to discuss the subject of the approaching Centenary of Methodism, which had for years been anticipated with great interest. With Mr. Butterworth— a Member of Parliament and a loyal Methodist and generous supporter of our funds—originated the idea of commemorating God's goodness in a fitting manner, not in a boastful spirit; a committee which had been appointed reported to the next Conference "that the primary object of the said celebration should be the religious and devotional improvement of the centenary"; and that there should also be "thank-offering to Almighty God" in money contributions for some of the institutions of the Church. The Conference approved these suggestions, and appointed a day of united prayer in January, 1839, "for the outpouring of the Holy Spirit" on the Connexion during the year.

There had been some difficulty in fixing the date of the birth of Methodism; but 1739 was determined on, because then the first class-meetings were held, the first chapel at Bristol was opened, the first hymn-book published; then the United Societies were formed, then field-preaching began, and then Whitefield, Charles Wesley, and others held that historic lovefeast in Fetter Lane when the Holy Spirit came so mightily on them that all were awed into silence, some sank down insensible, and on recovering they sang with one voice their Te Deum of reverent praise.

The centenary year being decided, a three days' convention of ministers and laymen was held at Manchester to make the needful arrangements; its proceedings were marked by a wonderful enthusiasm and liberality.

The Centenary Conference assembled at Liverpool in 1839. It could report an increase of 13,000 members. On August 5 it suspended its ordinary business for the centenary services—a prayer-meeting at six in the morning being followed by sermons preached by the Rev. Thomas Jackson and the President, the Rev. Theophilus Lessey. A few weeks later came the festal day, October 25, morning prayer-meetings and special afternoon and evening services being held throughout the country. Never had there been such large gatherings for rejoicing and thanksgiving; there were festivities for the poor and for the children of the day and Sunday schools. These celebrations, in which the whole Methodist Church joined, aroused the interest of the nation, and called forth appreciative criticism from press and pulpit.

When the idea of this first great Thanksgiving Fund was

originally contemplated, the most hopeful only dared look for L10,000; but when the accounts were closed the treasurers were in possession of L222,589, one meeting at City Road having produced L10,000; and the effort was made at a time of great commercial depression. This remarkable liberality drew the attention of the Pope, who said in an encyclical that *the heretics were putting to shame the offerings of the faithful.*

Not a few meetings took the form of lovefeasts, where generous giving proved the reality of the religious experiences; for there has ever been an intimate connexion between the fellowship and the finance of Methodism. Part of the great sum raised went to the Theological Institution, part to Foreign Missions; Wesleyan education was helped by a grant, L1,000 were paid over to the British and Foreign Bible Society; and the laymen desiring to help the worn-out ministers and their widows and children, L16,000 were set aside to form the Auxiliary Fund for this purpose.

It was now that the Missionary Committee were enabled to secure the Centenary Hall, the present headquarters of the Missionary Society. The remaining sums were given to other useful purposes.

Methodism in 1839 in all its branches [Footnote] reckoned more than 1,400,000 members, with 6,080 itinerant preachers and 350 missionaries; 50,000 pupils were instructed in the mission schools, and there were upwards of 70,000 communicants and at least 200,000 hearers of the gospel in Methodist mission chapels. In England alone the Wesleyan Methodists owned 3,000 chapels, and had many other preaching places; there were 3,300 Sunday schools, 341,000 scholars, and 4,000 local preachers. These figures, when, compared with those given at the end of our sketch, will furnish some idea of the numerical advance of Methodism throughout the world during the Queen's reign.

[Footnote: "Methodism in all its branches" must be understood of *all* bodies bearing the name of Methodist, including the New Connexion and the Primitive Methodists. The membership of Wesleyan Methodism alone throughout the world, according to the *Minutes of Conference* for 1839, was 1,112,519; and the total ministry, including 335 missionaries, 4,957.]

The centenary celebrations marked the high flood-tide of spiritual prosperity for many ensuing years, for a time of great trial followed. Gladly would we forget the misunderstandings of our fathers; yet this sketch would be incomplete without reference to unhappy occurrences which caused the loss of 100,000 members, and allowance must be made for this terrible loss in estimating the progress of Wesleyan Methodism. The troubles began when certain anonymous productions, known as "Fly Sheets," severely criticised the administration of Methodism and libellously assailed the characters of leading ministers, especially Dr. Bunting, who stood head and shoulders above all others in this Methodist war. He was chosen President when only forty-one, and on three other occasions filled the chair of the Conference. He became an authority on Methodist government and policy. Dr. Gregory says, "As an administrator, he was unapproached in sagacity, aptitude, personal influence, and indefatigability... his character was spotless." He was a born commander. The "Liverpool Minutes," describing the ideal Methodist preacher, are his work.

Dr. Bunting volunteered to be tried by the Conference as to the anonymous charges against him, but no one came forward with proofs to sustain them. Three ministers, Messrs. Everett, Dunn, and Griffiths, supposed to be the chief movers of this agitation, refused to be questioned on the matter, and defying the Conference, were expelled. Thereafter the agitation was kept up, and caused great disaffection in the Societies, resulting in the loss we have referred to. The seceders called themselves "Reformers"; many of them eventually joined similar bodies of seceders, forming with them the "United Methodist Free Churches." These in 1857 reported a membership of 41,000, less than half that which was lost to Wesleyan Methodism. But now they may be congratulated on better success, the statistics for 1896 showing, at home and abroad, a total of nearly 90,000 members, with 1,622 chapels, 417 ministers, 3,448 local preachers, 1,350 Sunday schools, and 203,712 scholars. It may be noted with pleasure that the leaders of the movement outlived all hostility to the mother Church; one of them attended the Ecumenical Conference of 1881, and took the sacrament with the other delegates.

With great regret we speak of this painful disruption, now that so much better feeling animates the various Methodist Churches. Practically there is no difference of doctrine among them. It has been well said, "Our articles of faith stand to-day precisely as in the last century, which makes us think that, like Minerva from the brain of Jupiter, they were born full-grown and heavily armoured."

An influential committee has been appointed to ascertain how concerted action may be taken by the Methodist Churches; and the hope is cherished that their suggestions may lead to the adoption of methods which will prevent strife and friction and unworthy rivalry. The New Connexion and Methodist Free Church Conferences also appointed a joint committee to consider the same subject. The brotherly desire for spiritual fellowship and mutual help and counsel thus indicated must be held as a very hopeful token of something better than numerical advance.

Anne E. Keeling

The bitter experiences through which the Church passed called attention to the need for modification and expansion of Wesleyan Methodist polity. The Conference of 1851 appointed a committee of ministers to consider the question; 745 laymen were invited to join them. Their recommendations led Conference to adopt resolutions defining the proper constitution of the quarterly meeting, and to provide for special circuit meetings to re-try cases of discipline, which had been brought before the leaders' meeting, when there was reason to think that the verdict had been given in a factious spirit. The chairman of the district, with twelve elected by the quarterly meeting, formed a tribunal to re-try the case. From this decision there was an appeal to the district synods, and also to the Conference. Provision was made for the trial of trustees, so that every justice should be done them. Local Church meetings were guaranteed the right of appeal to Conference, and circuits were allowed to memorialise Conference on Connexional subjects, within proper limits. The quarterly meetings, having considered these resolutions, gave them a cordial reception, and they were confirmed by the Conference of 1853.

No new rule is enforced by Conference until opportunity is given to bring it before all the quarterly meetings, and it is not likely to become Methodist law if the majority object. The enlarged district synods are an additional safeguard for the privileges of the people. By ballot the circuit quarterly meetings may now elect one, or in some cases two gentlemen, who, with the circuit steward, shall represent the circuit in the district synod.

In 1889, Conference sanctioned the formation of Methodist councils, composed of ministers and laymen, to consult on matters pertaining to Methodist institutions in the towns. Their decisions of course do not bind any particular Society.

The disaffection so fruitful of suffering had been due to a suspicion that men were retained in departmental offices when they no longer had the confidence of the people. Now such officials are only elected for six years, though eligible for re-election. One-sixth of the laymen on Connexional committees retire yearly; they may be re-elected, but must receive a four-fifths vote. Visitors may be present when the President is inducted into office, and during the representative session, when also reporters other than ministers are now allowed to take notes.

It was the year 1878 which witnessed that most important development of Methodist economy, the introduction of lay representatives to take part with ministers in the deliberations of Conference. This was no sudden revolution; laymen had long had their share in the work of quarterly meetings, district synods, and great Connexional committees; in 1861 they were admitted to the Committees of Review, which arranged the business of Conference; they sat in the nomination committee each year, and had power to scrutinise, and even to alter, the lists of names for the various committees. Now in natural sequence they were to be endowed with legislative as well as consultative functions; it might be said they had been educated to this end.

The committee appointed to consider the matter having done its work, the report was submitted to the district synods and then to Conference. Long, earnest, animated, but loving was the debate that ensued; the assembled ministers, by a large majority, determined that the laity should henceforth share in their deliberations on all questions not strictly pastoral.

It was resolved that there should be a representative session of 240 ministers and 240 laymen. The ministerial quota was to consist of President and secretary, members of the Legal Hundred, assistant secretary, chairmen of districts not members of the Hundred, and representatives of the great departments; six ministers stationed in foreign countries, but visiting England at the time; and the remainder elected by their brethren in the district synods; the laymen to be elected in the synods by laymen only. A small proportion at one Conference is chosen to attend the next.

Such were the new arrangements that came into force in 1878, causing no friction, since they secured "a maximum of adaptation with a minimum of change"; there was no difficulty in deciding what business should belong to either session of Conference. It is needless to dwell here on minor alterations, introduced in the past, or contemplated for the future, as to the order of the sessions; it may amply suffice us to remark that Wesleyan Methodism, thanks to the modifications of its constitution which we have briefly touched upon, is one of the most truly popular Church systems ever devised. For, as the Pastoral Address of 1896 puts it, "Methodism gives every class, every member, all the rights which can be reasonably claimed, listens to every complaint, asserts no exclusive privilege, but insures that all things are done 'decently and in order.'"

The great change just described, being the work of the ministers themselves, and accomplished by them before there was any loud demand for it, was effected with such moderation and discretion as not to entail the loss of a single member or minister. This was justly held a cause for great thankfulness; and it was determined to raise a thanksgiving fund for the relief of the various departments.

Great central meetings, extending over two years (1878—1880), were held throughout the country, and were characterised by enthusiasm and wonderful generosity. At a time when the country was suffering almost unheard of commercial depression, the sum of L297,500 was raised, to be apportioned between Foreign Missions, the Extension of Methodism in Great Britain, Education, Home Missions, Methodism in Scotland, the Sunday-school Union, a new Theological College, the "Children's Home," the Welsh and German chapels in London, a chapel at Oxford, the relief of necessitous local preachers, and the promotion of temperance. The missionary debt was paid, and the buildings for soldiers and sailors at Malta and Aldershot were cleared of debt.

Such work could not be done if the circuits acted independently; but united as they are, and forming one vast connexion, much which would otherwise be impossible can be achieved by means of the great Connexional funds. Of these funds not a few have been established since 1837; but the most important among them, the Foreign Mission fund, can boast an earlier origin.

Wesleyanism, indeed, is essentially missionary in spirit, her original aim being to spread scriptural holiness throughout the world. "The world is my parish," said Wesley though he himself could never visit the whole of that parish, his followers have at least explored the greater part of it, causing the darkness to flee before the radiance of the lamp of truth.

British Methodism has now missions in almost every quarter of the globe—in Asia, in Africa, on the Continent of Europe, in the Western Hemisphere. Her mission agencies include medical missions, hospitals, schools for the blind, homes for lepers, orphanages, training and industrial schools, etc.

In Europe we have set on foot missions in countries that are nominally Christian, where the people are too often the victims of ignorance, wickedness, vice, scepticism, and superstition; France, Germany, Austria, Italy, Spain, and Portugal have all been objects of our missionary enterprise

Anne E. Keeling

during the present reign, and in some instances conspicuous success has been attained. Witness the good work still going on in Italy, and the independent position attained by the *Conference, Methodiste de France*.

In India, Ceylon, China, and Burma, our agents are working amongst races in which they have to combat heathenism strong in its antiquity. The progress is necessarily slow, but a point has been reached where great success may be prophesied, as the result largely of the work of the pioneers. The schools are turning out many who, if they do not all become decided Christians, are intellectually convinced that Christianity is right, and will put fewer difficulties in the way of their children than they themselves had to contend with. This educational work prepares the way for the gospel; observers declare that nearly all converts in Ceylon have been trained in our schools.

The important missions in Southern and Western Africa must not be forgotten, nor those in Honduras and the Bahamas.

The present policy throughout our actual mission-field is as far as possible to raise up native agents. Probably the heathen lands will be won for the great Captain of salvation by native soldiers; but for a long time they will need officers trained in countries familiar for generations with the blessings of the gospel. The number of our missionaries may be stated at 400, more than half being native agents; there are 2,680 other mission workers, 52,058 Church members; 84,113 children and young people having instruction in the schools. But these figures would give a false idea of the progress of the work if compared with the statistics of 1837; for *then* our missions included vast regions that have now their own Conferences. When the Queen ascended the throne Fiji was a nation of cannibals. Two years before her accession our

Missionary Society commenced operations in those islands. John Hunt laboured with apostolic zeal, and died breathing the prayer, "God, for Christ's sake, bless Fiji, save Fiji." The prayer is already answered. All these islands have been won for Christ, and are trophies of Wesleyan missionary toil. There are 3,100 native preachers under the care of nine white missionaries; 1,322 chapels, 43,339 members and catechumens, and more than 42,000 scholars. Fiji has become almost a nation of Methodists. But it were vain to look for traces of this vast achievement in the "Minutes of Conference" of 1896; for a special feature of our missionary policy is the establishment of affiliated Conferences, which in course of time become self-supporting. In 1883 all the branches of the Canadian Methodists united to form one Canadian Conference. The first French Conference met in 1852. In 1855 the Conference of Eastern British America was formed. The same year the first Australian Conference met, and took charge of the Missions in Fiji, the Friendly Isles, and New Zealand. The first South African Conference met in 1882, and the two West Indian Conferences in 1884. Although more or less independent of the mother Conference, they still retain the characteristics of Methodism. A distinct branch of Mission work, known as the Women's Auxiliary, has been established, and sends forth ladies to engage in educational, zenana, and medical work. They are doing good service in India, China, and other parts of the world. In 1896 they expended more than L10,000.

The total expenditure last year (1896) was L124,700, incurred by our own Mission work and by grants to the affiliated Conferences. It is satisfactory to note that in the districts helped, including those covered by these Conferences, an additional L185,000 was raised. We have magnificent opportunities; and with full consecration of our people's wealth there would be glorious successes in the future. Foreign Missions have been the chief honour of

Methodism, and it is to be hoped the same affection for them will be maintained; for wherever Methodism is found throughout the world, it is the result of mission work.

Meanwhile there has been no sacrificing of home interests. Never were greater efforts made by Methodism for the evangelisation of the masses in Great Britain. The Home Mission Fund, first instituted in 1756, was remodelled in 1856. Its business is to assist the dependent circuits in maintaining the administration of the gospel, to provide means for employing additional ministers, and to meet various contingencies with which the circuits could not cope unassisted. Our needs as a Connexion demand such a Contingent Fund. One-third of the amount raised by the Juvenile Home and Foreign Missionary Association is devoted to Home Missions. The income, which in 1837 was less than L10.000, is now more than L36,000; an increase witnessing to a spirit of aggression and enterprise in modern Methodism. This fund provides for the support of the Connexional evangelists and district missionaries.

In the year 1882, under the head "Home Missions," there was a new and important departure, by the appointment of the first "Connexional evangelists," of whom there are now four; they have already been the means of great blessing throughout the country, showing that the old gospel, preached as in the old days, is still mighty to awaken and convert.

Under the direction of the Home Mission Committee, commissioners visit certain districts, to give advice and discover the best methods for improving the condition of Methodism where it appears to be low.

Special attention is given to the villages. The "Out-and-Out Band" subscribed for four Gospel Mission vans, each carrying two evangelists, and a large quantity of literature, to the villages; the evangelists in charge conducting services in the village chapels and in the open air. The sale of books and the voluntary contributions of the people help to defray the expenses. This agency is now under the direction of the Home Mission committee, and the gospel cars will be known as "Wesleyan Home Mission Cars."

Another new movement, helpful to village Methodism, is the "Joyful News" mission, originating with the Rev. Thomas Champness, who has been set free from ordinary circuit work to manage it. He trains lay agents, for whose services there is a great demand in villages where the people are too poor to maintain additional ministers, and where the supply of local preachers is deficient. Some of these agents are at work abroad.

The energetic Home Mission Committee has also set on foot missions where Methodism was feeble. Nor are those forgotten who "go down to the sea in ships, and do business in great waters." As far as means permit, efforts are made for the spiritual benefit of our sailors in all the great ports of the world; our soldiers, too, are equally cared for. Methodism has always been interested in the army, in which some of Wesley's best converts were found; yet there was no systematic work in it before 1839, when an order by the commander-in-chief permitted every soldier to attend the church of his choice. Some years afterwards, the Rev. Dr. Rule strove hard to secure the recognition of the rights of Wesleyans, and after much struggle the War Office recognised Wesleyan chaplains. The work and position of Wesleyan Methodism are now thoroughly organised throughout the world. The government allows a capitation grant for all declared Wesleyans, and it amounts to a large sum of money every year. In 1896 there were, including the Militia, 22,663 declared Wesleyans in the army and 1,485

Anne E. Keeling

Church members. There are 28 Sailors' and Soldiers' Homes, providing 432 beds, and these Homes have been established at a cost of L35,000. In them are coffee bars, libraries, lecture halls, and, what is most appreciated by Christian soldiers, rooms for private prayer. The officiating ministers, who give the whole or part of their time to the soldiers and their families, number 195.

There are many local preachers among the soldiers, and at least two have left the ranks to become ministers.

On the Mission field, soldiers render valuable aid to the missionary in building chapels, distributing tracts, and often teaching and preaching to the natives and others. Thus, whilst helping to hold the empire for their Queen, they are hastening on the day when all the kingdoms of the world shall be the kingdom of our Lord and of His Christ.

This deeply interesting work in the Army and Royal Navy is appropriately mentioned in connexion with our Home and Foreign Missions, both intimately concerned in its maintenance and management. It is right to mention that the Soldiers' and Sailors' Homes described are free to all members of H.M.'s sea and land forces, irrespective of religious denomination.

PART II

One great event in Methodist history since 1837 now calls for notice—the assembling of the first Oecumenical Conference in Wesley's Chapel, City Road, London, in 1861. This idea was in strict keeping with the spirit Wesley discovered when, five weeks before his death, he wrote to his children in America: "See that you never give place to one thought of separating from your brethren in Europe. Lose no opportunity of declaring to all men that the Methodists are one people in all the world, and that it is their full determination so to continue,

"'Though mountains rise, and oceans roll,
To sever us in vain.'"

The growing affection among Methodists of all branches made the idea of an Oecumenical Conference practicable.

The suggestion took form at the Joint Conference of the Methodist Episcopal Church of America in 1876. The American Methodists sent a delegate to the British Conference, proposing a United Conference which should demonstrate to the world the essential oneness in doctrine, spirit, and principle of all the Churches which historically trace their origin to John Wesley; such a manifestation, it was hoped, would strengthen and perpetuate that unity.

Further, the Conference was to discover how to adjust our mission work so as to prevent waste and friction; suggesting also modes and agencies for the most successful work of evangelisation. Nor was this all; its promoters trusted to gain light on the relation of universal Methodism to education, civil government, .other Christian bodies, and missionary enterprise at large, and looked for a vast increase in spiritual

Anne E. Keeling

power and intelligent, enthusiastic activity among the various branches of Methodism, whose gathering together might well draw "the attention of scholars and reformers and thinkers to the whole Methodist history, work, and mission," while a new impulse should be given to every good work, and a more daring purpose of evangelisation kindled. The British Conference pointed out the need of frankly recognising the not unimportant differences amongst the various Methodist bodies, so as to rule out of discussion any points which had a suggestion of past controversies. The American Conference accepted this.

The smaller Methodist bodies being invited to join, the four hundred delegates were sent up by the various branches of the Methodist Church as nearly as possible in proportion to their numerical strength; seven sections of British Methodism and thirteen from the United States and the Mission fields, numbering probably twenty millions, were represented. It was fitting that the first Oecumenical Conference should meet in City Road, the cathedral of Methodism. Bishop Simpson preached the opening sermon; the delegates then partook of the sacrament together, and Dr. Osborn, President of the Conference, gave the opening address. The Oecumenical Conference did not aim at determining any debated condition of Church membership, or at defining any controverted doctrine, or settling any question of ritual; it met for consultative, not legislative purposes. As such, the gathering brought about the thing which is written: "Thy watchmen shall lift up the voice; with the voice together shall they sing... Then thou shalt see, and flow together, and thine heart shall fear, and be enlarged."

By a happy coincidence, that largehearted son of Methodism, the late Sir William M'Arthur, was then Lord Mayor of London, and he gave a congratulatory welcome to the delegates at a magnificent reception in the Mansion House.

The next important event in Methodist history during the Queen's reign is the rise and progress of the great Wesleyan Missions in the towns—a vast beneficent movement, in which some at least of the aspirations cherished by the promoters of the first Oecumenical Conference appeared to have been realised.

The tendency of our day is towards a steady flow of population from the villages to the towns, especially to London. In 1837, there was only one London district, covering a very wide area, and including six circuits, whose total membership was only 11,460, after a hundred years of Methodism. The various branches of the recently established London Mission report more than a third of this number after less than ten years' labour.

The success of London Methodism in late years is largely due to the establishment of the Metropolitan Chapel Building fund in 1862. The late Sir Francis Lycett gave L50,000, on condition that an equal amount should be raised throughout the country, and that ten chapels, each seating at least a thousand persons, should in ten years be built in the metropolitan area. The noble challenge called forth a fit response. In his will he left a large sum to the same fund, so the committee could offer an additional L500 pounds to every chapel commenced before the end of 1898, with a proportionate grant to smaller chapels; aid will also be given by the committee in securing additional ministerial supply. Such offers should stimulate chapel building for the two years. Already, since the establishment of the fund, more than ninety chapels have been built in London at a cost of L630,000, towards which the fund contributed in grants and loans L213,000. Before 1862, there were only three important chapels south of the Thames, and now there are thirty-seven. During the last ten or twelve years unprecedented prosperity has been shown, not only in chapel

Anne E. Keeling

building, but in chapel filling, and the establishment of successful missions.

In 1885 the earnest attention of the Churches was directed to "outcast London." The deepest interest was aroused, especially in Methodist circles; and that year great meetings were held in City Road, to initiate a movement that should benefit London's outcasts. A large sum of money was raised, and the London Mission formed. The West London Mission at St. James's Hall, the East End branch, and the almost deserted chapel in Clerkenwell became notable centres. Thus at one time efforts were put forth to reach the rich, the artisans, and the outcasts. The success has abundantly justified the enterprise. In addition to evangelistic work, the missions make strenuous efforts to improve the social condition of the people, for Methodism realises that she is called to minister not only to the souls, but also to the bodies of men. Already, as a result of the London Mission, a new, fully organised circuit has grown up; the West London Mission alone reporting a membership which is one-tenth of the whole membership of London in 1837.

The latest and most novel branch of the work is the "Bermondsey Settlement," established six years ago in the poorest district of south-east London. In this hall of residence live devoted workers who have been trained in our universities or in our high-class schools, and who spend their leisure in benefiting their poor neighbours by religious, educational, and social effort. A home for women, in which about ten ladies reside, is connected with the settlement, which is in special connexion with Wesleyan schools throughout the country. The programme of work is extensive, and in addition the settlement takes an increasing part in local administration and philanthropy, many non-resident workers assisting.

To support the London Mission, appeal is made to Methodists throughout the country and the world. The meetings held on its behalf in the provinces have greatly blessed the people, stimulating them to fresh efforts in their own localities. Similar agencies had previously been established in various great trading centres, where the tendency is for the people who can afford it to leave the towns and to live in the suburbs. Thus many chapels have become almost deserted. The Conference decided that the best method of filling these chapels would be to utilise them as Mission halls, for aggressive evangelistic and social effort; which has been done with surprising success in Manchester, Leeds, Hull, Birmingham, and many other large towns. In Manchester there are from ten to twelve thousand people reached by the Mission agencies, and already a new circuit has been formed, the members of its Society having been gathered in from the army of distress and destitution. It would be impossible here to enumerate the thousand ways in which the Mission workers toil for the redemption of the downfallen, or to tell half the tale of their success. But all this work could not be so well carried on without the assistance of another important department. The Wesleyan Chapel Building Committee, instituted in 1818, was reconstituted in 1854; it meets monthly in Manchester to dispose of grants and loans, to consider cases of erections, alterations, purchases, and sales of Wesleyan trust property, and to afford advice in difficult cases. It has also to see that all our trust property is duly secured to the Connexion. The erection of the Central Hall in Manchester, to be at once the headquarters of our Chapel Committee and of the great Mission, marked a most important era in Methodist aggressive enterprise. The income of the Chapel Fund from all sources last year was L9,115. It was reported that the entire debt discharged or provided for during the last forty-one years was L2,389,073, and the total debt remaining on trust property is not more than L800,000; while L9,000,000

Anne E. Keeling

had been expended on chapel buildings during the thirty years preceding 1893.

The Extension of Methodism Fund was established in 1874, to supplement the ordinary funds of the Connexion and the local resources of the people, by aiding in the increase of chapel accommodation throughout the country, and in the extension of Methodism by Home Mission and similar agencies. At first the building of a thousand chapels was contemplated; but already 1,796 cases have been helped, with grants and loans amounting to L122,999. In 1867 a fund was started for the relief and extension of Methodism in Scotland; a Chapel Fund for the North Wales District was instituted in 1867, and for South Wales in 1873. There are now in Great Britain 10,000 Wesleyan chapels, which will accommodate 2,156,209 hearers, more than four times the number of members returned; for there is something misleading, as far as the general public is concerned, in the published statistics of Methodism, which take account of class-meeting membership only. Estimating the other Methodist bodies at the same rate, Methodist chapels provide accommodation for 3,000,000 people; so that the united Methodist Church in this country is second only to the Established Church of England.

The Wesleyan Methodist Trust Assurance Company was established in 1872, for the insurance of Methodist Trust property only. The Board of Trustees for Chapel Purposes was formed in 1866, which undertakes to invest money intended for the chapel trust and for Methodist objects. Seeing that there are so many funds in Methodism, and that while some have a balance, others might be obliged to borrow at a high rate of interest, it was suggested that a Common Cash Fund should be established, making it possible for the committees to borrow from and lend to one another, the borrowers paying the ordinary bank rate of interest, and the profits being equally divided among the funds.

A passing reference must be made to another committee, instituted in 1803—the Committee of Privileges and Exigency: and in 1845 an acting special committee for cases of great emergency was formed. Between the sessions of the Conference this committee often renders great service, safeguarding Methodist interests when they would be endangered by proposed government measures, or in any other way. At present it is engaged in trying to get through Parliament several measures in the interests of Nonconformity generally.

The subject of education drew the anxious attention of Wesley; his followers were less alive to its importance, until just before the Queen came to the throne. The training of the ministry was neglected, and the young ministers had to educate themselves. Though Wesley approved the idea of a seminary for his preachers, it was only three years before the Queen's accession that the first Theological Institution was opened at Hoxton. The Centenary Fund provided for one such institution at Richmond, and another at Didsbury. The Headingley branch was opened in 1868, and the Birmingham branch, built with part of the Thanksgiving Fund, in 1881. Our ministers are now far better trained than were the old Methodist preachers, and, taking them as a whole, they do not come short of their predecessors in any necessary qualification for their work.

Their culture must not be judged by the scantiness of their literary production. The empress Catherine once said to a French *savant*, "My dear philosopher, it is not so easy to write on human flesh as on paper." Much more difficult is the task of our ministers, whose religious, social, and financial work leaves them little of that learned leisure

Anne E. Keeling

enjoyed by Anglican divines, who by their masterly works have made the entire Christian Church their debtor. But in the period we are reviewing, despite the demands made on the time of the ministers, many have written that which will not easily be forgotten. The Church that nurtured Dr. Moulton, whose edition of Winer's "Greek Grammar" is a standard work, used by all the greatest Greek New Testament scholars, need not be ashamed of her learning. Dr. Moulton and Dr. Geden were on the revision committee which undertook the fresh translation of the Old and New Testaments. Other Wesleyan ministers have made their mark as commentators, apologists, scholars, and scientists in the last few decades. The *Fernley Lectures* have proved the ability of many Methodist preachers; we lack space to refer to the many able writers who have ceased from their labours.

The *London Quarterly Review* has kept up the literary reputation of Methodism: nor are we behind any Nonconformist Church in journalistic matters. Two newspapers represent the varying shades of opinion in Methodism, and give full scope to its expression. A high level of excellence is seen in the publications of the Book Room, and our people when supporting it are also helping important Connexional funds, to which the profits are given.

While increasing care has been taken with the training of the ministry, lay education has not been neglected. Kingswood School, founded by Wesley, continues, as in his day, to give excellent instruction to ministers' sons. In 1837 a Methodist school, Wesley College, was opened at Sheffield, and a few years later one at Taunton, well known as Queen's College. The Leys School at Cambridge, under the head-mastership of Dr. Moulton, was opened in 1874, and has shown "the possibility of reconciling Methodist training with the breadth and freedom of English public school life." There are in Ireland excellent colleges at Belfast and Dublin.

In 1875, a scheme for establishing middle-class schools was adopted, resulting in the opening of such schools at Truro, Jersey, Bury St. Edmunds, Woodhouse Grove, Congleton, Canterbury, Folkestone, Trowbridge, Penzance, Camborne, and Queenswood; all report satisfactorily.

Elementary education, which has made such great progress during the Queen's reign, engaged the anxious attention of our authorities long before the initiation of the School Board system, under which the average attendance in twenty-five years increased almost fourfold. Methodism has been in the forefront of the long battle with ignorance.

The establishment of "week-day schools" in connexion with this great Church owed its origin to the declaration of the Conference in 1833. that "such institutions, placed under an efficient spiritual control, cannot fail to promote those high and holy ends for which we exist as a religious community." The object was to give the scholars "an education which might begin in the infant school and end in heaven," thus subserving the lofty aim of Methodism, "to fill the world with saints, and Paradise with glorified spirits"; a more ambitious idea than that expressed by Huxley when he said, "We want a great highway, along which the child of the peasant as well as of the peer can climb to the highest seats of learning."

In 1836 the attention of the Conference was directed to education in general, and especially to Wesleyan day schools; the Pastoral Address of 1837, regretting that children had to be trained outside the Church or be left untaught, expressed the hope that soon, in the larger circuits, schools might be established which would give a scriptural and Wesleyan education. Already some schools had been commenced; and the plan was devised which has been the basis of all subsequent Methodist day-school work.

Anne E. Keeling

In 1840 it was decided to spend the interest of the L5,000 given from the Centenary Fund for the training of teachers, work which was at first carried on at Glasgow. The determination of Conference to perfect its plan of Wesleyan education was quickened when an unfair Education Bill, not the last of its kind, was introduced into Parliament in 1843, proposing to hand over the children in factory districts to the Church of England. An Education Fund was established. Government, in 1847, offered grants for the training of elementary school teachers; and in 1851 the Westminster Training College was opened, with room for 130 men students. In 1872, in response to an increased demand for Wesleyan teachers, a separate college for mistresses was opened at Southlands, Battersea. Already four thousand have been trained in these institutions. Many hold positions in Board schools. In 1896 the number in Wesleyan and Board schools was 2,400.

The system thus inaugurated met a great and real need, and under it excellent work has been done on the lines laid down by the Department at Whitehall; for, receiving State aid, the training colleges and all the schools, like other similar denominational institutions on the same footing, are inspected and in a measure controlled by the national educational authority. In 1837 there were only 31 Wesleyan day schools; to-day there are 753 school departments, and on their books 162,609 scholars. But the introduction of free education has made it difficult for the Methodist Church to maintain her schools, efficient though they be. Since 1870, when school boards were introduced, the number of Wesleyan day schools has only increased by 10, while 9,752 Board schools have arisen, and the Church of England schools have increased from 9,331 to 16,517; the Roman Catholic schools actually trebling in number and attendance.

In view of these changed conditions, Conference has

expressed itself anxious for such a complete national system of education as might place a Christian unsectarian school within reasonable distance of every family, especially in rural districts, with "adequate representative public management"; it has most earnestly deprecated the exclusion of the Bible, and suitable religious instruction therefrom by the teachers, from the day schools; but, so long as denominational schools form part of the national system, it is resolved to maintain our schools and Training Colleges, in full vigour. Difficulties, undreamed of sixty years ago, surround this great question; but assuredly Methodism will be true to its trust and its traditions.

The cost of Wesleyan schools last year was L215,634, and was met by school fees, subscriptions, and a government grant of L185,780. The Education Fund of 1896, amounting to L7,115, was spent on the Training Colleges, grants to necessitous schools, etc.

Wesley approved of Sunday schools as means of giving religious instruction to the children of the poor, and Hannah Ball at High Wycombe, a good Methodist, and Silas Told, teaching at the Foundery, both anticipated the work of Raikes by several years. In 1837 there were already 3,339 Sunday schools, with 341,442 scholars. Today the schools number 7,147, the officers and teachers 131,145, and there are in the schools 965,201 children and young people. The formation in 1869 of the Circuit Sunday-school Union, and in 1874 of the Connexional Sunday-school Union, has done much for the schools, in providing suitable literature for teachers and scholars, and in organising their work. An additional motive to Scripture study is furnished by the "Religious Knowledge Examinations" instituted by Conference; certificates, signed by the President, being granted to teachers and scholars who succeed in passing the examinations. In recognition of the value of so important a department of the Church, adequate representation at the quarterly meetings is now accorded to the Sunday schools.

It is not in our day only that the pastoral oversight of the young has been deemed worthy of attention; the duty has always been enforced on ministers; but in 1878 there were first formed junior Society classes, to prepare children for full membership. There are now seventy-two thousand in such classes.

In 1896 we note a new effort to bring young people into the kingdom, in the foundation of the "Wesley Guild," of which the President of Conference is the head, with four vice-presidents, two being laymen. The guild is "a union of the young people of a congregation. Its keynote is comradeship, and its aim is to encourage the young people of our Church in the highest aims of life." The story of its origin may be briefly told.

The Rev. Charles H. Kelly introduced the subject in the London Methodist Council, and then brought the matter before the Plymouth Conference of 1895, dwelling on the desire existing to form a Wesley Guild that should do for Britain what the Epworth League does for American Methodism, and secure the best advantages not only of that league, but of the Boys' Brigade, Bands of Hope, Christian Endeavour and Mutual Improvement Societies, which it should federate. The Liverpool Conference of 1896 therefore sanctioned the formation of the "Wesley Guild." Its three grades of members include young people already attached to the Church, with others not yet ripe for such identification, and "older people young in heart," who all join in guild friendship, and aid in forming this federation of the existing societies interesting to young people.

By periodical meetings, weekly if possible, for devotional,

social, and literary purposes, a healthy common life and beneficent activity are stimulated, and the rising generation is happily and usefully drawn into relation with the older Church workers, whom it aids by seeking out the young, lonely, and unattached, and bringing them into the warm circle of youthful fellowship.

Such in brief is the programme of the Guild, which may yet greatly enrich the Church with which it is connected.

We turn now to one of the most notable changes in Methodism during the Queen's reign—the wonderful advance in the temperance movement. Wesley himself was an ardent temperance reformer, but his preachers were slow to follow him. A few prominent men strove long to induce Conference to institute a temperance branch of our work, and finally succeeded, their efforts having effected a great change in opinion. For many years our theological students, though not compelled thereto, have almost all been pledged abstainers. 1873 saw Conference appoint a temperance committee "to promote legislation for the more effectual control of the liquor traffic—and in general for the suppression of intemperance." In 1879 a scheme was sanctioned for the formation of Methodist Bands of Hope and Circuit Temperance Unions; and a special Sunday, the last in November, is devoted to considering "the appalling extent and dire result" of our national sin, one of the greatest obstacles to that "spread of scriptural holiness" which is the aim of the true Wesleyan Methodist, whose chosen Church, with its manifold organisation, has unequalled facilities for temperance work. In 1896 the report showed 1,374 temperance societies, with 80,000 members—figures that do not include all the abstainers in Methodism; some societies have no temperance association, and some Methodists are connected with other than our own temperance work. The 4,393 Bands of Hope count 433,027 members.

Anne E. Keeling

We have already spoken of the growth and development of social philanthropic work in connexion with the great Methodist missions in towns; there remains one most important movement in this direction to notice—the establishment of the "Children's Home," which, begun in 1869 by Dr. Stephenson, received Conference recognition in 1871. It has now branches in London, Lancashire, Gravesend, Birmingham, and the Isle of Man, and an emigration depot in Canada. Over 900 girls and boys are in residence, while more than 2,900 have been sent forth well equipped for the battle of life; some of them becoming ministers, local preachers, Sunday-school workers, and in many ways most useful citizens. The committee of management has the sanction of Conference. This "powerful arm of Christian work" not only rescues helpless little ones from degradation and misery; it undertakes the special training of the workers amongst the children in industrial homes and orphanages; and hence has arisen the institution in 1895 of the order of Methodist deaconesses, which is recommended by Conference to Connexional sympathy and confidence, the deaconesses rendering to our Church such services as the Sisters of Mercy give to the Church of Rome. One example may suffice. A London superintendent minister describes the work of one of the Sisters during the past twelvemonth as "simply invaluable. She has visited the poor, nursed the sick, held services in lodging-houses, met Society classes and Bible-classes, gathered round her a godly band of mission-workers, and in a hundred ways has promoted the interests of God's work."

Two events made 1891 memorable for Methodists, the centenary of Wesley's death and its commemoration being the first.

The Conference decided that suitable memorial services should be held, and an appeal made to Methodists everywhere for funds to improve Wesley's Chapel and the graveyard containing his tomb. Universal interest was aroused; all branches of Methodism were represented; the leading ministers of Nonconformist Churches also shared in the services. Crowded and enthusiastic congregations assembled in City Road when on Sunday, March 1, the Rev. Charles H. Kelly, Ex-President, preached on "The Man, his Teaching, and his Work," and when the Rev. Dr. Moulton delivered the centenary sermon. On March 2, a statue of Wesley was unveiled—exactly one hundred years after his death—Dean Farrar and Sir Henry H. Fowler addressing the meeting.

The Allan Library, the gift of the late Thomas R. Allan, containing more than 30,000 books and dissertations, was opened by the President; it has since been enriched by gifts of modern books from the Fernley Trustees and others, and a circulating library is now connected with it. Accessible on easy terms to ministers and local preachers, and within the reach of many others, this library should be a useful stimulus to the taste for study among ministers and people.

The other event of the year was the meeting of the second Oecumenical Conference in October, at Washington, in the country where Methodism obtained great triumphs. The Conference lasted twelve days, like its predecessor; the opening sermon, prepared by the Rev. William Arthur, was read for him, Mr. Arthur's voice being too weak to be heard; and the President of the United States gave a reception at the Executive Mansion, and also visited the Conference. Many topics of deep interest were discussed on this occasion, and not the least attractive subject was the statistical report presented. The difficulty of estimating the actual strength and influence of Methodism is very great.

In the present year the membership of the Wesleyan

Methodists, for Great Britain and Ireland, is estimated at 494,287; of other Methodist bodies in the United Kingdom at 373,700; the affiliated Conferences of Wesleyan Methodists in France, South Africa, the West Indies, and Australasia at 212,849, being 1,942 for France, 62,812 for South Africa, 50,365 for the two West Indian, and 97,730 for the Australasian Conferences. American Methodism in all its branches, white and coloured, returns a membership of 5,573,118, while the united Methodism of Canada shows 272,392, and the foreign missions of British Wesleyan Methodism 52,058 members. These figures, giving a total of 6,978,404 members, exclusive of the ministers, estimated at 43,368, are sufficiently gratifying; yet they do not represent the real strength of the Church at large, and give only a faint idea of its influence.

The Oecumenical Report gave the number of Methodist "adherents" as 24,899,421, intending, by the term *adherents*, those whose religious home is the Methodist chapel, though their visits to it be irregular. For the British Wesleyans the two millions of sittings were supposed to represent the number of adherents (yet should all the occasional worshippers wish to attend at once, it may be doubted if they could be accommodated); for the other branches of Methodism in the United Kingdom, four additional persons were reckoned to each member reported. The statistics for Ireland and Canada were checked by the census returns. Probably in the case of missions the adherents would be more than four times the membership. Varying principles were adopted for the United States, and the adherents reckoned at less than four times the members reported. Should we to-day treat the returns of membership on the same principle (Sunday scholars being now as then included in the term "adherents "), we should find nearly thirty millions of persons in immediate touch with Methodism and strongly bound to it. Compare these figures with those of

1837, and we must exclaim, "What hath God wrought!"

Estimating the increase of British Methodism, we have to remember that the population has almost doubled in the sixty years, while British Wesleyan Methodism has not doubled; but the great losses occasioned by the agitations must be taken into account, and also the curious fact that the ratio of increase for Methodism at large, in the ten years between the two Oecumenical Conferences, was thirty per cent—twice as great as the increase of population in the countries represented; the Methodist Church in Ireland actually increasing thirteen per cent, while the population of the country was diminishing and the other Protestant Churches reported loss.

If the increase in Great Britain be proportionally smaller, this need not cause surprise, in view of that vast development of energy in the Established Church which is really due to the reflex action of Methodism itself; that Church, with all the old advantages of wealth and prestige and connexion with the universities and grammar schools which she possessed in the days of her comparative supine-ness, with her clergy roll of 23,000, and her many voluntary workers, having in twenty-seven years almost doubled the number of her elementary schools, largely attended by Methodist children. But the indirect influence of Methodism is such as cannot be represented in our returns; figures cannot show us the true spiritual status of a Church. The total cost of the maintenance of our work in all its branches can be estimated; and so able an authority as the Rev. Dr. H. J. Pope stated it at from L1,500,000 to L1,750,000 pounds annually, a sum more than equal to a dividend on fifty millions of consols; but it is impossible to compute the profit to the human race from that expenditure and the work it maintains. This may be said with certainty, that other Churches have been greatly enriched thereby. We may just refer to that remarkable religious movement, the Salvation Army, of Methodist origin, though

Anne E. Keeling

working on new lines; doing such work, social and evangelistic, as Methodism has chosen for its own, and absorbing into its ranks many of our own trained workers. "The Salvationists, taught by Wesley," said the late Bishop of Durham, "have learned and taught to the Church again the lost secret of the compulsion of human souls to the Saviour."

"The Methodists themselves," says John Richard Green, "are the least result of the Methodist revival"; the creation of "a large and powerful and active sect," numbering many millions, extending over both hemispheres, was, says Lecky, but one consequence of that revival, which exercised "a large influence upon the Established Church, upon the amount and distribution of the moral forces of the nation, and even upon its political history"; an influence which continues, the sons of Methodism taking their due part in local and imperial government. Eloquent tributes to the work of Wesley are frequent to-day, the *Times*, in an article on the centenary of his death, saying: "The Evangelical movement in the Church of England was the direct result of his influence and example, and since the movements and ideas which have moulded the Church of England to-day could have found no fitting soil for their development if they had not been preceded by the Evangelical movement, it is no paradox to say that the Church of England to-day is what it is because John Wesley lived and taught in the last century.... He remains the greatest, the most potent, the most far-reaching spiritual influence which Anglo-Saxon Christianity has felt since the days of the Reformation." So far the *Times*, of him whom it styles "the restorer of the Church of England." Many impartial writers, some being ardent friends of the English Church, have also recognised a gracious overflow from Methodism which has blessed that Church, the Nonconformist bodies, and the nation at large. If a man would understand "the religious history of the last hundred years," that "most important ecclesiastical fact of modern times," the rise and progress of Methodism, must be studied in relation to the Anglican and the older Nonconformist Churches, and the general "missionary interests of Christianity": so we are taught by Dr. Stoughton, who has traced the influence of Methodism in the general moral condition of the country and the voluntary institutions of our age. The doctrines once almost peculiar to Wesley and his followers —such as entire sanctification—are now accepted and taught by many Churches, and the religious usages of Methodism are imitated, watchnight services being held, and revival mission services and prayer-meetings being conducted, in Anglican churches; while the hymns of Charles Wesley, sung by all English-speaking Protestants, and translated into many languages, enrich the devotional life of the Christian world.

It was a fit tribute to the benefits which the English Church has derived from the Methodist movement, when the memorial tablet to the brothers John and Charles Wesley was unveiled in Westminster Abbey by the late Dean Stanley, in 1872.

"The bracing breezes," said Dr. Stoughton, "came sweeping down from the hills of Methodism on Baptist meadows as well as upon Independent fields." We may give some few instances that will show what blessings have come to Nonconformist Churches by the agency of Methodism.

A remarkable incident that occurred in 1872 was recorded in the *Wesleyan Methodist Magazine*. Dr. Jobson had invited five eminent ministers to meet the President of Conference at his house. After breakfast their conversation quite naturally took the form of a lovefeast, all being familiar with Methodist custom; when Dr. Allon, Dr. Raleigh, and Dr. Stoughton all said they were converted in Methodist chapels, and began Christian work as Methodists. Thomas Binney said that "the direct instrumentality in his conversion was Wesleyan," and Dr. Fraser was induced to enter the ministry by a Wesleyan lady. Charles H. Spurgeon was converted through the instrumentality of a Primitive Methodist local preacher; William Jay of Bath was converted at a Methodist service; John Angell James caught fire among the Methodists; and Thomas Raffles was a member of the Wesleyan Society; Dr. Parker began his ministrations as a Methodist local preacher; while Dr. Dale has shown the indebtedness of Nonconformity to Methodism. In France and Germany Methodist agency has been one of the strongest forces in re-awakening the old Protestant Churches; the services held by our Connexional evangelists send many converts to swell the fellowship of Churches not our own. And the same effects followed the great Methodist revival in America; out of 1,300 converts, 800 joined the Presbyterian and other denominations. But while calling attention to the spiritual wealth and the beneficent overflow of Methodism, we would not be unmindful of the debt which Methodism owes to other Churches, and in special of its obligations to those Anglican divines of our day who have enriched the whole Church of Christ by their scholarly contributions to sacred literature; and we would ascribe all the praise of Methodist achievement to the almighty Author of good, whom the spirit of ostentation and vain glorifying must displease, while it would surely hinder His work.

The great desire of Methodism to-day—its great need, as Dr. Handles expressed it in his presidential address—is "fulness of spiritual life." If this be attained, the actual resources of the Church will amply suffice to carry on its glorious future mission; it will not fail in its primary duties of giving prominence to the spirituality of religion, of maintaining strict fidelity to scriptural doctrine, of giving persevering illustration of the fellowship of believers, nor in upholding the expansion of home and foreign missions, nor in ceaseless efforts to promote social advancement. "There is no rigid system of Church mechanism, nor restraining dogma," to hinder missions.

At present four-sevenths of the human race are in heathen darkness. To win the world for Christ demands that Methodists should unite with all His true soldiers. Wesley said: "We have strong reason to hope that the work He hath begun He will carry on until the day of the Lord Jesus; that He will never intermit this blessed work of His Spirit until He has fulfilled all His promises, until He hath put a period to sin and misery, infirmity and death, re-established universal holiness and happiness, and caused all the inhabitants of the earth to sing, 'Alleluia: for the Lord God omnipotent reigneth.'" If Methodism be faithful to her mission, this prophecy may be fulfilled.

When the second temple was built, Haggai exhorted Zerubbabel and Joshua to be strong, and all the people to be strong, and to work, for the Lord was with them. Let Methodists be strong in God's strength, and work with the consciousness that the Lord of hosts is with them, and they will insure success to the great mission of their Church.

We will conclude with the last paragraph of the Rev. Charles H. Kelly's sermon at the celebration of the centenary of Wesley's death in 1891.

"Surely the lesson to the Methodists of to-day is clear enough. Let us cherish the memory of our forefathers, let us emulate their spirit, let us cling to their God-given doctrines, let us cultivate, as they did, communion with the Master and fellowship with each other. Let us aim to be one, to do our duty. Let us strive to make our Church a greater power for evangelism among the people of the earth than ever, let us look to the Holy Spirit for the richer baptism of grace, and

Methodism, so blest of the Lord in the past, will yet be blest. Her mission is not accomplished, her work is not done; long may she live and prosper. Peace be within her walls, and prosperity within her palaces. For my brethren and companions' sake, the faithful living and the sainted dead, I will now say, Peace be within her; peace be within her."

CONCLUSION

The last days of the half-century are fleeting fast as we write, and we are yet at peace with Europe, as when Victoria's reign began. How long that peace shall last, who shall say? who can say how long it may be ere the elements of internal discord that have threatened to wreck the prosperity of the empire, shall be composed to a lasting peace, and leave the nation free to follow its better destiny? But foes within and foes without have many times assailed us in vain in past years; many times has the political horizon been shadowed with clouds portending war and strife no less gloomily than those which now darken it, and as yet the Crimean war is the only war on which we have entered that can be called European; many times have grave discontents broken our domestic peace, but wise statesmanship has found a timely remedy. We need not, if we learn the lessons of the past aright, fear greatly to confront the future. Not to us the glory or the praise, but to a merciful overruling Providence, ever raising up amongst us noble hearts in time, that we are found to-day

"A nation yet, the rulers and the ruled,"

not quite bankrupt in heart or hope or faith, but possessing

"Some sense of duty, something of a faith,

Anne E. Keeling

        Some reverence for the laws ourselves have made,
        Some patient force to change them when we will;"

and we may justly acknowledge, in thankfulness not vainglorious, the happier fate that has been ours above many another land, that may still be ours, "if England to itself do rest but true."

We have seen during these sixty years the map of Europe remodelled to an undreamed of extent. Fair Italy, though still possessing her fatal gift of beauty, though still suffering many things, is no longer the prey of foreign unloved rulers, but has become a nation, a mere "geographical expression" no longer; Germany, whose many little princedoms were once a favourite theme of British mockery, is now one great and formidable empire; the power of Russia has, despite the Crimean check, continued to expand, while desperate internal struggles have shaken that half-developed people, proving fatal to the gentle successor of Nicholas, the emancipator of the Russian serfs, and often threatening the life of *his* successors; and the once formidable American slave-system has been swept away, with appalling loss of human life; a second President of the United States has fallen by the hand of an assassin; and new difficulties, scarce inferior to those connected with slavery, have followed on its abolition. Our record shows no calamity comparable to the greatest of these, if we set aside the Indian horrors so terribly avenged at the moment, but by their teaching resulting ultimately in good rather than evil.

Besides the furious strife and convulsion that have rent other lands, how inconsiderable seem the disturbances that disfigure our home annals, how peaceful the changes in our constitutional system, brought about orderly in due form of law, how purely domestic the saddest events of our internal history! We wept with our Sovereign in her early widowhood, a bereavement to the people as well as to the Queen; we trembled with her when the shadow of death hung over her eldest son, rejoicing with her when it passed away; we shared her grief for two other of her children, inheritors of the noble qualities of their father, and for the doom which took from us one whom we had loved to call "our future king"; we deplored the other bereavements which darkened her advancing years; we have lamented great men taken from us, some, like the conqueror of Waterloo, "the great world-victor's victor," in the fulness of age and honour, others with their glorious work seemingly half done, their career of usefulness mysteriously cut short; we have shuddered when the hateful terrorism, traditional pest of Ireland through centuries of wrong and outrage, has once and again lifted its head among ourselves; we have suffered—though far less severely than other lands, even than some under our own rule—from plague, pestilence, and famine, from dearth of work and food. But what are these woes compared to those that other peoples have endured, when it has been said to the sword, "Sword, go through the land," and the dread word has been obeyed; when war has slain its thousands, and want its tens of thousands; or when terrible convulsions of nature have shaken down cities, and turned the fruitful land into a wilderness?

Events have moved fast since the already distant day when the Colonial and Industrial Exhibition was ministering exultation to many a British heart by its wonderful display of the various wealth of our distant domains and their great industrial resources. We were even then tempted—as have been nations that are no more—to pride ourselves on having reached an unassailable height of grandeur. Since then our territory has expanded and our wealth increased; but with them have increased the evils and the dangers inseparable from great possessions, and the responsibilities involved in them. We can only "rejoice with trembling" in this our

Anne E. Keeling

second year of Jubilee. Remembering with all gratitude how we have been spared hitherto, and mindful of the perils that wait on power and prosperity, let it be ours to offer such sacrifices of thanksgiving as can be pleasing to the almighty Ruler of the ways of men, whom too often in pride of power, in selfish satisfaction with our own achievements, we forget.

Many are the works of mercy, well pleasing in His sight, with which we can associate ourselves, even in this favoured land, whose ever increasing wealth is balanced by terrible poverty, and its affluence of intellectual and spiritual light by grossest heathen darkness. Day by day, as our brief account has shown, are increasing efforts put forth by our Christian men and women to overcome these evils; and through such agencies our country may yet be saved, and may not perish like other mighty empires, dragged down by its own over-swollen greatness, and by neglect of the eternal truth that "righteousness exalteth a nation: but sin is a reproach to any people."

Choose from Thousands of 1stWorldLibrary Classics By

A. M. Barnard
Ada Leverson
Adolphus William Ward
Aesop
Agatha Christie
Alexander Aaronsohn
Alexander Kielland
Alexandre Dumas
Alfred Gatty
Alfred Ollivant
Alice Duer Miller
Alice Turner Curtis
Alice Dunbar
Allen Chapman
Alleyne Ireland
Ambrose Bierce
Amelia E. Barr
Amory H. Bradford
Andrew Lang
Andrew McFarland Davis
Andy Adams
Angela Brazil
Anna Alice Chapin
Anna Sewell
Annie Besant
Annie Hamilton Donnell
Annie Payson Call
Annie Roe Carr
Annonaymous
Anton Chekhov
Archibald Lee Fletcher
Arnold Bennett
Arthur C. Benson
Arthur Conan Doyle
Arthur M. Winfield
Arthur Ransome
Arthur Schnitzler
Arthur Train
Atticus
B.H. Baden-Powell
B. M. Bower
B. C. Chatterjee
Baroness Emmuska Orczy
Baroness Orczy
Basil King
Bayard Taylor
Ben Macomber
Bertha Muzzy Bower
Bjornstjerne Bjornson

Booth Tarkington
Boyd Cable
Bram Stoker
C. Collodi
C. E. Orr
C. M. Ingleby
Carolyn Wells
Catherine Parr Traill
Charles A. Eastman
Charles Amory Beach
Charles Dickens
Charles Dudley Warner
Charles Farrar Browne
Charles Ives
Charles Kingsley
Charles Klein
Charles Hanson Towne
Charles Lathrop Pack
Charles Romyn Dake
Charles Whibley
Charles Willing Beale
Charlotte M. Braeme
Charlotte M. Yonge
Charlotte Perkins Stetson
Clair W. Hayes
Clarence Day Jr.
Clarence E. Mulford
Clemence Housman
Confucius
Coningsby Dawson
Cornelis DeWitt Wilcox
Cyril Burleigh
D. H. Lawrence
Daniel Defoe
David Garnett
Dinah Craik
Don Carlos Janes
Donald Keyhoe
Dorothy Kilner
Dougan Clark
Douglas Fairbanks
E. Nesbit
E. P. Roe
E. Phillips Oppenheim
E. S. Brooks
Earl Barnes
Edgar Rice Burroughs
Edith Van Dyne
Edith Wharton

Edward Everett Hale
Edward J. O'Biren
Edward S. Ellis
Edwin L. Arnold
Eleanor Atkins
Eleanor Hallowell Abbott
Eliot Gregory
Elizabeth Gaskell
Elizabeth McCracken
Elizabeth Von Arnim
Ellem Key
Emerson Hough
Emilie F. Carlen
Emily Bronte
Emily Dickinson
Enid Bagnold
Enilor Macartney Lane
Erasmus W. Jones
Ernie Howard Pie
Ethel May Dell
Ethel Turner
Ethel Watts Mumford
Eugene Sue
Eugenie Foa
Eugene Wood
Eustace Hale Ball
Evelyn Everett-green
Everard Cotes
F. H. Cheley
F. J. Cross
F. Marion Crawford
Fannie E. Newberry
Federick Austin Ogg
Ferdinand Ossendowski
Fergus Hume
Florence A. Kilpatrick
Fremont B. Deering
Francis Bacon
Francis Darwin
Frances Hodgson Burnett
Frances Parkinson Keyes
Frank Gee Patchin
Frank Harris
Frank Jewett Mather
Frank L. Packard
Frank V. Webster
Frederic Stewart Isham
Frederick Trevor Hill
Frederick Winslow Taylor

Friedrich Kerst
Friedrich Nietzsche
Fyodor Dostoyevsky
G.A. Henty
G.K. Chesterton
Gabrielle E. Jackson
Garrett P. Serviss
Gaston Leroux
George A. Warren
George Ade
Geroge Bernard Shaw
George Cary Eggleston
George Durston
George Ebers
George Eliot
George Gissing
George MacDonald
George Meredith
George Orwell
George Sylvester Viereck
George Tucker
George W. Cable
George Wharton James
Gertrude Atherton
Gordon Casserly
Grace E. King
Grace Gallatin
Grace Greenwood
Grant Allen
Guillermo A. Sherwell
Gulielma Zollinger
Gustav Flaubert
H. A. Cody
H. B. Irving
H.C. Bailey
H. G. Wells
H. H. Munro
H. Irving Hancock
H. R. Naylor
H. Rider Haggard
H. W. C. Davis
Haldeman Julius
Hall Caine
Hamilton Wright Mabie
Hans Christian Andersen
Harold Avery
Harold McGrath
Harriet Beecher Stowe
Harry Castlemon
Harry Coghill
Harry Houidini

Hayden Carruth
Helent Hunt Jackson
Helen Nicolay
Hendrik Conscience
Hendy David Thoreau
Henri Barbusse
Henrik Ibsen
Henry Adams
Henry Ford
Henry Frost
Henry James
Henry Jones Ford
Henry Seton Merriman
Henry W Longfellow
Herbert A. Giles
Herbert Carter
Herbert N. Casson
Herman Hesse
Hildegard G. Frey
Homer
Honore De Balzac
Horace B. Day
Horace Walpole
Horatio Alger Jr.
Howard Pyle
Howard R. Garis
Hugh Lofting
Hugh Walpole
Humphry Ward
Ian Maclaren
Inez Haynes Gillmore
Irving Bacheller
Isabel Cecilia Williams
Isabel Hornibrook
Israel Abrahams
Ivan Turgenev
J.G.Austin
J. Henri Fabre
J. M. Barrie
J. M. Walsh
J. Macdonald Oxley
J. R. Miller
J. S. Fletcher
J. S. Knowles
J. Storer Clouston
J. W. Duffield
Jack London
Jacob Abbott
James Allen
James Andrews
James Baldwin

James Branch Cabell
James DeMille
James Joyce
James Lane Allen
James Lane Allen
James Oliver Curwood
James Oppenheim
James Otis
James R. Driscoll
Jane Abbott
Jane Austen
Jane L. Stewart
Janet Aldridge
Jens Peter Jacobsen
Jerome K. Jerome
Jessie Graham Flower
John Buchan
John Burroughs
John Cournos
John F. Kennedy
John Gay
John Glasworthy
John Habberton
John Joy Bell
John Kendrick Bangs
John Milton
John Philip Sousa
John Taintor Foote
Jonas Lauritz Idemil Lie
Jonathan Swift
Joseph A. Altsheler
Joseph Carey
Joseph Conrad
Joseph E. Badger Jr
Joseph Hergesheimer
Joseph Jacobs
Jules Vernes
Julian Hawthrone
Julie A Lippmann
Justin Huntly McCarthy
Kakuzo Okakura
Karle Wilson Baker
Kate Chopin
Kenneth Grahame
Kenneth McGaffey
Kate Langley Bosher
Kate Langley Bosher
Katherine Cecil Thurston
Katherine Stokes
L. A. Abbot
L. T. Meade

L. Frank Baum
Latta Griswold
Laura Dent Crane
Laura Lee Hope
Laurence Housman
Lawrence Beasley
Leo Tolstoy
Leonid Andreyev
Lewis Carroll
Lewis Sperry Chafer
Lilian Bell
Lloyd Osbourne
Louis Hughes
Louis Joseph Vance
Louis Tracy
Louisa May Alcott
Lucy Fitch Perkins
Lucy Maud Montgomery
Luther Benson
Lydia Miller Middleton
Lyndon Orr
M. Corvus
M. H. Adams
Margaret E. Sangster
Margret Howth
Margaret Vandercook
Margaret W. Hungerford
Margret Penrose
Maria Edgeworth
Maria Thompson Daviess
Mariano Azuela
Marion Polk Angellotti
Mark Overton
Mark Twain
Mary Austin
Mary Catherine Crowley
Mary Cole
Mary Hastings Bradley
Mary Roberts Rinehart
Mary Rowlandson
M. Wollstonecraft Shelley
Maud Lindsay
Max Beerbohm
Myra Kelly
Nathaniel Hawthrone
Nicolo Machiavelli
O. F. Walton
Oscar Wilde

Owen Johnson
P.G. Wodehouse
Paul and Mabel Thorne
Paul G. Tomlinson
Paul Severing
Percy Brebner
Percy Keese Fitzhugh
Peter B. Kyne
Plato
Quincy Allen
R. Derby Holmes
R. L. Stevenson
R. S. Ball
Rabindranath Tagore
Rahul Alvares
Ralph Bonehill
Ralph Henry Barbour
Ralph Victor
Ralph Waldo Emmerson
Rene Descartes
Ray Cummings
Rex Beach
Rex E. Beach
Richard Harding Davis
Richard Jefferies
Richard Le Gallienne
Robert Barr
Robert Frost
Robert Gordon Anderson
Robert L. Drake
Robert Lansing
Robert Lynd
Robert Michael Ballantyne
Robert W. Chambers
Rosa Nouchette Carey
Rudyard Kipling
Saint Augustine
Samuel B. Allison
Samuel Hopkins Adams
Sarah Bernhardt
Sarah C. Hallowell
Selma Lagerlof
Sherwood Anderson
Sigmund Freud
Standish O'Grady
Stanley Weyman
Stella Benson
Stella M. Francis

Stephen Crane
Stewart Edward White
Stijn Streuvels
Swami Abhedananda
Swami Parmananda
T. S. Ackland
T. S. Arthur
The Princess Der Ling
Thomas A. Janvier
Thomas A Kempis
Thomas Anderton
Thomas Bailey Aldrich
Thomas Bulfinch
Thomas De Quincey
Thomas Dixon
Thomas H. Huxley
Thomas Hardy
Thomas More
Thornton W. Burgess
U. S. Grant
Upton Sinclair
Valentine Williams
Various Authors
Vaughan Kester
Victor Appleton
Victor G. Durham
Victoria Cross
Virginia Woolf
Wadsworth Camp
Walter Camp
Walter Scott
Washington Irving
Wilbur Lawton
Wilkie Collins
Willa Cather
Willard F. Baker
William Dean Howells
William le Queux
W. Makepeace Thackeray
William W. Walter
William Shakespeare
Winston Churchill
Yei Theodora Ozaki
Yogi Ramacharaka
Young E. Allison
Zane Grey

www.ingramcontent.com/pod-product-compliance
Lightning Source LLC
Chambersburg PA
CBHW031351170626
46807CB00002B/921